The Psychgeist of Pop Culture

The Psychgeist of Pop Culture
Stranger Things

Anton Roberts

Play Story Press

Contents

Copyright © by Play Story Press 2024
Pittsburgh, PA
https://playstorypress.org/
ISBN: 978-1-300-96953-2 (Print)
ISBN: 978-1-300-96363-9 (Digital)
DOI: https://doi.org/10.17613/67f2-g219

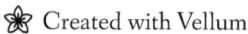 Created with Vellum

PSYCHGEIST

Psychgeist Of Pop Culture Series

Play Story Press
Pittsburgh, PA

Series Editor: Rachel Kowert, PhD

Over the last few decades interest in pop psychology has grown faster than our Netflix backlogs. This series highlights iconic pop culture content from television, film, literature, and video games through an examination of the psychological mechanisms that endear us to these stories for a lifetime.

SERIES TITLES

The Witcher (2023), edited by Rachel Kowert, PhD
The Mandalorian (2024), edited by Jessica E. Tompkins, PhD
The Umbrella Academy (2024), edited by Arienne Ferchaud, PhD
Bluey (2024), edited by Kelli Dunlap, PsyD
Stranger Things (2024), edited by Anton Roberts

Chapter 1

Welcome to the Upside Down

Anton Roberts

"It's more about this juxtaposition between ordinary and extraordinary. These friendships of various generations of people coming together to fight something extraordinary, and the awe and the fear that comes with that."

-Duffer Brothers, Creators of Strangers Things[1]

Stranger Things premiered on *Netflix* in July 2016 and is the creative brainchild of the Duffer Brothers. Taking inspiration from David Lynch, Stephen King, Wes Craven, and H. P. Lovecraft, among others, *Stranger Things* is perhaps best described as an investigative drama, with supernatural elements, wrapped in a bow of nostalgia for the popular culture of 1980s America. In many ways, the show is a typical coming of age story that primarily focuses on the adventures of the teenage inhabitants of a fictional, suburban town of Hawkins, Indiana. However, that is where the "typical" storytelling stops. From government conspiracies, secret labs, and alternative dimensions to first kisses, teenage love, and a side of Dungeons and Dragons – this show has a little bit of everything.

Since its release, it has been immensely popular with critics and mainstream audiences alike, cementing itself as an iconic, nostalgic representation of American culture. It has been nominated for, and won, a host of awards including a Screen Actors Guild Award for best Ensemble Cast in a Drama Series, a Peabody Award for Best Entertainment Program, and 11 Emmy Awards in various categories. In 2023, *Stranger Things* was crowed the most viewed English-speaking series in Netflix's history[2].

Within the pages of this book, you will find a collection of essays exploring what lies beyond the surface (and even in the upside down) of *Stranger Things*, diving deeper into the stories of Mike, Will, Lucas, Max, Dustin, and Eleven, as well as some of the wider cast of characters from Hawkins, Indiana (RIP Eddie).

In the end, our hope is that the words on these pages will shed some new light on to why the stories and characters of this series resonate with so many of us and provide a deeper and more nuanced understanding of the phenomenon that is *Stranger Things*.

---

1. Lewis, T. (2023, December 10). The Duffer Brothers: "The last series of Stranger Things is the biggest it's ever been." The Observer. https://www.theguardian.com/tv-and-radio/2023/dec/10/the-duffer-brothers-last-series-stranger-things-theatre-first-shadow-interview#:~:text=(For%20what%20it

2. ibid

Chapter 2

'Be Kind, Rewind'

Nostalgia and the Past
Saiqa Butt

N ostalgia can be many things: wistfulness, regret, rose-tinted reminiscence...what it is not, is accurate memory. This chapter will discuss the phenomenon of nostalgia in the context of *Stranger Things* as it provides a profound illustration of nostalgia, not just for those who lived through the 1980s, but also for younger generations experiencing this era second-hand.

What is Nostalgia?

Nostalgia can be described as a feeling that evokes a feeling of kindship or sense of 'coming home'. It is a sentimental longing or sense of affection for something, someone, or some time that has passed. The word itself is a compound Greek word nostos (return home) and algia (longing), coined by Johannes Hofer, a medical student treating the anxieties displayed by Swiss mercenaries fighting away from home. Feelings of nostalgia can be unintentionally triggered by music, (e.g., a song that was popular when you were in high school), smells (e.g., the scent of your mom's cooking), or sounds (e.g., the creak of a floorboard in an old house) or be purposely evoked. For instance, by looking through an old shoe box of photographs or watching a *Netflix* series steeped in iconography from a past era.

In modern psychology, is often defined as a sentimental longing or wistful affection for the past, typically accompanied by fond memories and a desire to return to or recreate moments from one's personal history[1]. From a philosophical perspective, nostalgia is seen as a complex and multifaceted relationship between the past, memory, and human consciousness. Philosophers place more emphasis on the temporal, or time, dimension of nostalgia, particularly how nostalgia reflects the way humans perceive and relate to time. Specifically, it has been argued that nostalgia highlights the human tendency to anchor oneself in the past which raises questions about the nature of our mortality and the significance of the past in shaping our identities. Regardless of the perspective, nostalgia is often regarded as a powerful emotion that arises when individuals reminisce about past experiences, people, or places. While generally seen as a positive experience, the emotions associated with this feeling are more accurately described as bittersweet, combining joy and sorrow, which would herald back to its original association with homesickness.[2]

While nostalgic memories are very much *real* for those experiencing them, it is important to note that they are not always *accurate* reflections of the past. *For* years, scholars have explored this tension between authentic recollections of the past and idealized or distorted versions of it, finding that nostalgic memories are often a selective and romanticized view of history, prompting inquiries into the accuracy of our memories and the role of nostalgia in constructing personal and collective histories. Regardless of their accuracy, nostalgia has been found to be influential in shaping societies and cultures as a powerful force in collective memory, influencing art, literature, politics, and societal attitudes towards progress and tradition[3].

Taken together, nostalgia can be thought of as an intricate interplay between memory, emotion, time, authenticity, and the human experience. It offers a lens through which we can explore the ever-

enduring allure of the past and its significance in shaping our understanding of self, society, and the world. As nostalgia is both a yearning
for, and idealization of, the past it is perhaps unsurprising then that
many of us feel bittersweet emotions when we feel nostalgic.

The Ideal versus Real of Nostalgic Memory

One of the interesting features about nostalgia is that despite the fact
they tap into *real* memories and emotions, they do not necessarily tap
into *accurate* ones. This idealisation is a common aspect of nostalgic
memories as we, as humans, tend to remember the past as better than
it was. For example, many of the nostalgic elements of 'Stranger
Things' represent an idealised version of the past, rather than an
accurate representation[4]. The show presents the 1980s as a time of
innocence and simplicity, yet this overlooks the complexities and
challenges of the era. In the United States alone there was civil
discontent, worries of nuclear war, a homelessness epidemic, the
erosion of the middle class, in addition to several wars on the other
side of the world that ran throughout the decade.

The selective memory aspect of nostalgia serves a purpose: it
offers comfort and escape, a daydream to get lost in. The bittersweet-
ness of it all. In the case of *Stranger Things,* this daydream-like
quality is tapped into through its major plot point: a group of young
people fighting against a greater evil, a battle that adults cannot fully
comprehend or engage with. This oversimplified narrative offers a
return to a time when life seemed simpler, and the lines between
good and evil, right and wrong, were more clearly drawn. The
monsters in the show are not just physical entities, but also represent
the childhood nightmares and fears, echoing the universal experience
of growing up.

It is also worth noting that the Duffer Brothers themselves are
aware of their portrayal of the "ideal" as compared to "real" reality of
the 1980s. They themselves have discussed in interviews that they
wanted to use 1980s America as their backdrop so they could *"fill*

this new world they created with their 80s childhood memories, adding a real sense of genuine nostalgia to lives led by the band of kids which become wrapped up in the show's mystery[5].

The Phenomenon of 'Second-Hand' Nostalgia

'Anemoia' was first coined by John Koenig in 2014, in his Dictionary of Obscure Sorrows, a collection of work that was developed in an attempt to expand the English language to provide terms for emotions that we have as yet to find names for. Anemoia is defined by Koenig as *'nostalgia for a time you've never known'.*[6] That is, having the bittersweet nostalgic feelings "second-hand", for a time, place, or person you have not directly experienced. In the case of *Stranger Things*, the feelings of "second-hand" nostalgia are pervasive.

As discussed in an op-ed from *London Runway*: *'For many Gen Zs and late Millennials, we may be feeling this strange sense of sentimentality because we are, by being placed in the middle of Hawkins, reliving our past in some sense. Looking at Barb and Nancy in their 'mom' jeans may actually remind us of the very person who is symbolised by such clothing – our mums!*[7]

Thus, despite the fact the show is set in the 1980s, many of the viewers of the show were born after the era it depicts. Despite this, many viewers express feeling a sense of sentimentality when watching the show. This is anemoia – the unique form of nostalgia not based on personal memories but on a collective idealisation of a past era. *Stranger Things* taps into a 'common consciousness', a shared yearning for the 'good old days', even among viewers who did not personally experience the hair, fashion, and music of the 1980s.

Nostalgia and Stranger Things

Stranger Things transports viewers to the 1980s, a decade marked by iconic movies, music, and fashion. The show whole heartedly embraces the '80s aesthetic in its storyline, soundtrack, visuals and sensory memories (oh the taste of a toasted Eggo in the morning). It pays homage to this era by featuring references to classic films like *E.T. the Extra-Terrestrial* (1982) and *The Goonies* (1985) and incorporates a synth-heavy soundtrack reminiscent of the period's music. This deliberate choice of setting and style taps into the 'rose-tinted' reminiscence of both older viewers who experienced the 1980s first-hand and younger audiences who have a romanticized view of the decade. Put another way, *Stranger Things* allows people to relive and celebrate their memories and cultural touchstones from the past, while also introducing these elements to new generations.

As mentioned earlier, nostalgia often revolves around a sense of familiarity and comfort. By setting the series in the 1980s, the world of *Stranger Things* feels familiar and inviting to those who grew up in that era. A time when kids rode their bikes around the neighbourhood and communicated through walkie-talkies. Many believe that one the key components to the success of 'Stranger Things' is due to the way it leans into the nostalgia of 1980s small town America[8]. Even though the Duffer Brothers have created publicly stated that they do not believe it to be the reason, or sole driver, for the audience connecting with it so profoundly[9], it certainly plays an element for viewers in the enjoyment of the show[10,11]. For many viewers, the show becomes more than just a series; it becomes a happy, rose-tinted exercise into the past. From the music choices to the production design, every detail is meticulously crafted to transport viewers back in time. This immersion enhances the viewing experience and makes it easier for viewers to become emotionally invested in the story.

Stranger Things encourages viewers to revisit or discover the cultural touchstones of the 1980s. Many viewers may be inspired to watch classic films, listen to '80s music, or explore the fashion and technology of the era, extending their engagement with the show beyond the screen. The shared nostalgia for the 1980s creates a sense of community among Stranger Things fans. Viewers often discuss and bond over their favourite references and moments from the show, fostering a sense of belonging and connection with others who share their appreciation for the era, and contributing to the longevity of "Stranger Things." As new generations discover the show and become captivated by these elements, it continues to attract a broad and dedicated fanbase. The enduring popularity of the series is a testament to the enduring power of nostalgia in pop culture.

Let's explore some of the different ways *Stranger Things* taps into the sense of nostalgia.

Nostalgia in Character Development

In Stranger Things, nostalgia plays a significant role in shaping the characters and their development. The show's young protagonists, including Eleven, Mike, Dustin, and Lucas, are all products of their 1980s upbringing. They are portrayed as kids who have a deep knowledge of and reverence for the pop culture of their time, from *Dungeons & Dragons,* X-men*, to *Star Wars*. We see this in the range of Star Wars toys in the show, and even the memorable scene in Season 1 where Eleven is asked to levitate the Millennium Falcon to prove her telekinetic abilities. Or in the not-so-subtle choice for Dustin to name his long-range radio 'Cerebro', the device used by Charles Xavier in the *X-men* comic series, to detect humans and mutants.

The way in which items or things from the 1980s are tied into character development is also notable. For example, Eleven's fondness for Eggo waffles, which she discovers in Mike's house, becomes a recurring motif throughout the series. Eggos, a popular, and iconic, waffle brand, were a staple in many American households during the 1980s. Their prominent placement in Stranger Things, a show set in the 1980s, instantly evokes a sense of that era. Eleven's affinity for Eggos creates an emotional connection for the audience. Her child-like enjoyment of this simple food resonates with viewers who might remember similar uncomplicated pleasures from their own childhoods. Do you remember a time when you were utterly obsessed with a specific food item? A taste, a texture, a smell that meant joy, safety, and peace? We connect with Eleven by sharing her emotional response to her favourite food Eggos become a recurring symbol throughout the series. This not only serves as a character trait for Eleven but also as a cultural reference point that audiences, especially those who grew up in, or are fond of, the 1980s, can instantly recognise and relate to.

The use of Eggos in Stranger Things also taps into a broader trend of 1980s nostalgia in media and marketing. By integrating a well-known product from that time, the show effectively blurs the line between past and present, appealing to both older viewers who experienced the 1980s first-hand and younger audiences drawn to the retro aesthetic. Beyond this, Eggos also serve as a plot device within the show, symbolizing Eleven's innocence and her connection to the "normal" world, contrasting with her otherwise traumatic and extraordinary experiences. Eggos in Stranger Things are more than just a product placement; they are a nostalgic emblem that resonate with viewers, enhance character development, and enrich the 1980s setting of the series. The sensory aspects of Stranger Things play a crucial role in its nostalgic appeal. The tastes, smells, and sounds of the 1980s are vividly recreated to tantalise the viewer. Interestingly, according to CNN Business[12], by giving Eggos 'cultural relevance', Stranger Things helped the aging brand in boosting its sales considerably.[13] Eleven's attachment to this simple breakfast food is a poignant reminder of her limited exposure to the outside world and her longing for a normal childhood.

Similarly, Mike's walkie-talkie, a symbol of communication and adventure in the 1980s, becomes a crucial tool for the group's communication and plays a significant role in the plot. As is the characters' interactions with the supernatural and their ability to navigate dangerous situations are influenced by their exposure to 1980s science fiction and horror films. They draw on their knowledge of these genres to devise strategies and make sense of the strange occurrences in their town. This is referenced best in the way the characters from the show interpret threats as creatures from Dungeons and

Dragons (e.g. the Demogorgon), where all manner of attributes are assumed based on the strength and limitations of the creature within the game. There is also the reference to *Nightmare on Elm Street*, in the episode 'The Bathtub' (S1, E7) a call back to an iconic scene in the movie. The heroes attempt to trick the Demogorgon in the same vein as the characters attempted to do so with Freddie Krueger, in the horror classic. This strategy is actually referenced explicitly with Dustin yelling "Elm Street" over the radio. These kinds of references also formed the foundation of the iconic, fan-favourite scene, where Dustin sings the theme song of the classic 1984 movie, *The Neverending Story*.

Nostalgia in Plot Development

Nostalgia is not limited to character development; it also influences the overall plot of Stranger Things. The show's central mystery, the disappearance of Will Byers and the appearance of a mysterious girl with supernatural powers, is shrouded in the mystery typical of the era's popular culture. As the characters search for Will and uncover the truth about the government experiments at Hawkins National Laboratory, they encounter elements of science fiction, horror, and conspiracy that are reminiscent of 1980s films and television series created around the rumours and conspiracy theories of clandestine government plans and cover ups, such as the Roswell crash and subsequent perceived 'hush up' by the government. The plot of Stranger Things is driven by a sense of nostalgia for classic adventure stories, where a group of kids embarks on a quest to save their friend and uncover hidden secrets. This narrative structure echoes the themes of friendship and camaraderie found in films like *The Goonies* and *Stand by Me*.

The supernatural threat in Stranger Things takes the form of a parallel dimension known as the Upside Down. This eerie and dark world is a nod to the alternate realities and otherworldly dimensions often found in 1980s science fiction and horror films, think '*Alien*',

E.T.' and, a personal favourite, 'Short Circuit' to name just a few. The Upside Down is both a source of terror and a vehicle for exploring the unknown, further emphasizing the show's nostalgic connection to the era.

The show's use of elements such as the role-playing game *Dungeons & Dragons*, also influences the characters' decision-making and problem-solving, adding a layer of complexity to the plot. In Season 4 (the most recent season of the show at the time of this writing), the game of *Dungeons & Dragons* being played by the Hellfire Club reflects the narrative being told over the entirety of the season. This meta type of storytelling is not only interesting for plot development, but another example of nostalgia being weaved into the very foundation of the show's plot.

There are various other clear parallels to the stories told in *Stranger Things* and classic movies of the past. For example, Eleven's story in the beginning of the series to Spielberg's classic 1980s movie *E.T., as* she dresses up in Mike's sister's clothing, she learns the ways of the world through the TV. [14] There are also numerous parallels between Stranger Things and Spielberg's *Close Encounters of the Third Kind.* There is an obvious comparison between the characters of Will Byers and Barry Guiler, particularly with the famous so-called "door scene" where both protagonists open the door to reveal the existential alien threat lurking beyond.

Nostalgia in Sound

Perhaps the most notable way the Duffer Brothers have tapped into a sense of nostalgia with *Stranger Things* is through the use of sound. The original score, composed by Kyle Dixon and Michael Stein, heavily uses synthesizers typical of the 1980s. This choice of instrumentation is reminiscent of the soundtracks from 80s movies and video games, further enhancing the show's nostalgic feel. The synth music is not just a background element; it's a deliberate and potent nod to the era's pop culture. The soundtrack of the show also features a wide array of popular music from the 1980s era. Songs from artists like The Clash, Joy Division, Toto, and others not only set the scene but also resonate with viewers who grew up in, or are familiar with, that period.

This layering of music with other 1980s visual elements (e.g., wardrobe, set design) has a powerful way of evoking emotions and memories. For example, the familiar tunes and stylistic choices of the soundtrack can trigger personal memories and feelings from the past, including nostalgia[15]. For younger viewers or those less familiar with the 1980s, the soundtrack serves as an introduction to the music and mood of the era. As mentioned earlier in this chapter, this can create a form of 'second-hand nostalgia', where viewers develop a reminiscent feeling for a time they didn't personally experience, but experience and enjoy this through their parents' nostalgia. A powerful demonstration of which was the use of Kate Bush's 'Running up that hill', and its incredible climb back to the top of the 100 Billboard after Episode four of Season four aired, showing us quite clearly how much of an emotional resonance Stranger Things and its use of soundtrack can evoke.

The Emotional Impact of Nostalgia

By immersing viewers in the sights, sounds, and culture of the 1980s, the show triggers a range of emotions, including joy and even a sense of loss, even in the way it portrays adolescence itself. For example, in Season 4, we see the characters go off to college to become 'adults'. This is juxtaposed with Will's childlike desire to maintain the 'party' at all costs - this reflects a very real human tension around growing up and the bittersweet emotions it evokes. Many viewers of Stranger Things who grew up in the 1980s or have a fondness for that era experience a sense of joy and nostalgia while watching the show. The familiar music, fashion, and technology evoke memories of their own childhoods and create a warm and comforting feeling, such as spending quality time outside with your friends in an era before the internet as we now know it, and the dangers of social media that followed. The show's portrayal of children on the cusp of adolescence, embarking on adventures and forming close friendships, taps into a longing for the innocence and simplicity of youth. Viewers may find themselves yearning for a time when life was less complicated and filled with wonder.

Nostalgia often prompts viewers to reflect on how times have changed since the 1980s. The show's portrayal of a small town during transformation, both socially and technologically, can lead viewers to consider the ways in which society has evolved over the years. It also reminds us of the constant and ever speeding change that we see, of how quickly the rural landscape changes, and the fear that we hold of that change. We see how quickly the things that were stables in our lives, such as VHS tapes and going to rent a film with the family on a Friday night, can become relegated to an outdated past, and us along with it. The fear of change only secondary to its speed, we feel our lives passing us by, finding ourselves in the 'modern' era, making us feel uncertain of our place within it. Alongside the feelings of nostalgia and joy, Stranger Things can also evoke a sense of loss. The show reminds viewers that the 1980s are a bygone era, and the passage of time is inevitable. This sense of loss can be particularly poignant for those who have a deep attachment to the decade.

Concluding Thoughts

Stranger Things masterfully utilises the lens of childhood to evoke nostalgia. The group of young, nerdy, and brave friends at the heart of the show offers a grittier, more adventurous version of the classic Enid Blyton gang. This portrayal allows viewers to live vicariously through these characters, experiencing the 1980s as they do. The show encapsulates the ideal of childhood – the excitement, the fear, the joys of simple pleasures like candy and video games, and the vivid imagination that makes everything seem possible and terrifying at the same time The relatable and well-developed characters in Stranger

Things create a strong emotional connection with viewers. As viewers follow their journeys and struggles, they become emotionally invested in the characters' fates.

Stranger Things also demonstrates the enduring power of nostalgia to transport viewers to a different time and evokes a complex mix of emotions. It reminds us that it is not merely a sentimentality for the past, but a potent tool for storytelling and audience engagement. In an ever-changing world, the ability to revisit and relive the past through the lens of pop culture provides comfort, connection, and a sense of belonging for viewers of all ages. It is a powerful example of how pop culture can evoke a sense of nostalgia, not only in those who have directly experienced a particular time but also in those who have not. It taps into a collective consciousness and a universal desire for a return to a simpler, more innocent time. Through its sensory-rich portrayal of the 1980s, the idealisation of childhood, and the comforting escape it offers from the complexities of modern life, Stranger Things demonstrates the multifaceted nature of nostalgia and its enduring appeal in our popular culture.

---

1. Batcho, K (PhD), Does nostalgia have a psychological purpose? https://www.apa.org/news/podcasts/speaking-of-psychology/nostalgia
2. Malpas, J (2011), Philosophy's Nostalgia by Jeff Malpas, https://philpapers.org/rec/MALPNI
3. Malpas, J (2011), Philosophy's Nostalgia by Jeff Malpas, https://philpapers.org/rec/MALPNI
4. Breier, D. G. (2022, May 27). "Stranger Things" and the frustrations of Gen X's '8os nostalgia habit. *Salon.* Retrieved from https://www.salon.com/2022/05/27/stranger-things-and-the-frustrations-of-gen-xs-8os-nostalgia-habit/
5. Balen, C. The strange case of 'Stranger Things' nostalgia, https://londonrunway.co.uk/the-strange-case-of-stranger-things-nostalgia/#:~:text=The%20Duffer%20Brothers%20wanted%20to,up%20to%20the%20mid%2D7os.
6. Koenig, J, The Dictionary of Obscure Sorrows, https://www.dictionaryofobscuresorrows.com/post/105778238455/anemoia-n-nostalgia-for-a-time-youve-never
7. Balen, C. The strange case of 'Stranger Things' nostalgia, https://londonrunway.co.uk/the-strange-case-of-stranger-things-nostalgia/#:~:text=The%20Duffer%20Brothers%20wanted%20to,up%20to%20the%20mid%2D7os.
8. Lu, R. (2022, July 28). The Nostalgic Genius of Stranger Things. *American*

Institute for Economic Research. Retrieved from https://www.aier.org/article/
the-nostalgic-genius-of-stranger-things/

9. Contreras, C, Why Stranger Things is more than just its nostalgic references, https://www.eonline.com/news/1331995/the-duffer-brothers-respond-to-stranger-things-criticism

10. Richardson, & Romero. (2018). Familiar Things: *Stranger Things*, Adolescence, and Nostalgia. *PsyArt*, 22, 95 – 104.

11. Hassler-Forest, D. (2020). 'When you get there, you will already be there': Stranger Things, Twin Peaks and the nostalgia industry. *Science Fiction Film & Television*, 13(2), 175-197.

12. Meyersohn, N. 'Stranger Things' caused an Eggo boom. Now sales are waffling, https://money.cnn.com/2018/06/20/news/companies/stranger-things-eggo-waffles-kellogg/index.html

13. Meyersohn, N. 'Stranger Things' caused an Eggo boom. Now sales are waffling, https://money.cnn.com/2018/06/20/news/companies/stranger-things-eggo-waffles-kellogg/index.html

14. White, B., Stranger Things Easter Eggs from season 1, https://decider.com/2019/06/18/stranger-things-season-1-easter-eggs/

15. Garrido, S., & Davidson, J. W. (2019). *Music, nostalgia and memory*. Berlin: Springer International Publishing.

Chapter 3

Mind over Monsters

Dungeons and Dragons and Mental Health in the Upside Down and Beyond
Jennifer Russell, MSW

I n *Stranger Things*, the main characters' immersion into the world of Dungeons and Dragons (D&D) serves as more than just a recreational activity; it mirrors their real-world experiences. Examining the narrative through a metaphorical lens of the Upside Down and alternate dimensions, the events of the show become intricately intertwined with the group's D&D sessions. This dual narrative approach not only enhances the thematic depth of the series but also provides a therapeutic lens through which viewers can explore the characters' collective and individual journeys in navigating complex social landscapes and real-world challenges.

Throughout the series, we witness the transformative journeys of Mike, Will, Lucas, Dustin, Eleven, and Max as they transition from childhood into young adulthood while confronting both real and narrative-driven monsters. The psychological zeitgeist of the show provides viewers with a unique window into the intricacies of childhood development, exposing the ruptures and repairs inherent in navigating the evolving landscape of close relationships. Despite the characters' individual growth and shifts away from storytelling games, the shared experience of their basement D&D sessions remains a unifying factor. As the primary characters mature, they unwittingly implement, and hone essential life skills acquired around the tabletop among their circle of friends. Beyond its portrayal in the show, what makes D&D truly special is its role as a relatable and secure haven for numerous self-proclaimed nerds and geeks alike, offering a space to explore both themselves and the world since its debut in 1974.

A Short History of Geek Culture

In the early-to-mid 20th century, a time when science fiction and fantasy literature captivated the imaginations of individuals seeking refuge in otherworldly realms, what is often referred to today as "geek culture" began to take form. Pioneering authors like J.R.R. Tolkien, Isaac Asimov, and H.P. Lovecraft laid the groundwork for what would later become the cornerstone of this phenomenon. Additionally, the emergence of comic books in the 1930s and 1940s, featuring iconic characters like Superman and Batman, further solidi-fied the foundations of this blossoming subculture.

The term "geek" was first recorded in 1915-1920 and was likely a variant of the German word *geck*, meaning "fool". In the first half of the 20th century, "geek" was the word used to describe a circus sideshow performer meant to put on horrifying spectacles for the audience, like biting the heads off small live animals[1]. Moving through the decades, a gradual change in meaning began to occur with the slang use of "geek" emerging in popular culture of the 1980s to describe a subculture of young, technologically savvy youth. Similarly, the term "nerd" gained popularity in the same time frame to describe unpopular, overly intellectual, young people who were interested in science or math[2].

Historically, geeks and nerds were not considered cool by main-stream society's standards. Both terms were used to denote social outcasts. The stereotypical image of school-aged boys playing Dungeons and Dragons in their parent's basement comes to mind, much like that depicted in the opening scene of Season 1, Episode 1 of *Stranger Things*.

With the continued emergence of and need for technology, these former outcasts became increasingly useful to society[3]. Geeks, then began adopting the term for themselves, proud of their standing in an emerging computer-based subculture[4]. A growing interest in science-fiction and fantasy, comic books, and role-playing games emerged and demonstrating knowledge of or devotion to these interests became a form of social currency between self-proclaimed geeks[5].

Dungeons and Dragons in *Stranger Things*

Dungeons and Dragons (D&D) is a collaborative storytelling role-playing game where players form an adventuring group, known as a "party", made up of created, often highly detailed characters, with the goal of exploring fantasy worlds together while embarking on epic quests[6]. Characters are typically created following pre-existing character class guides.

One group member is known as the Dungeon Master (DM), portrayed by Mike in earlier seasons and later by Eddie Munson within the Hellfire Club. The Dungeon Master organizes the adventure and supervises all aspects of the game, excluding the actions of the player characters. The Dungeon Master's role also encompasses resolving any internal conflicts between party members.

In the preface of the 2018 version Dungeons and Dragons Players Handbook, Mike Mearls describes how the game, in addition to strengthening friendships and creativity, D&D can help build the confidence to create and share. "D&D is a game that teaches you to look for the clever solution, share the sudden idea that can overcome a problem, and push yourself to imagine what could be, rather than simply accept what is[7]", a theme observed repeatedly throughout the seasons of *Stranger Things*.

The Party

Stranger Things begins in 1983 in the small town of Hawkins, Indiana, a mere 9 years after D&D's inception. Season 1, Episode 1 opens with Mike, Dustin, Lucas, and Will approaching the climax of a Dungeons and Dragons session in Mike's basement. In this opening scene, the party is animatedly arguing over how to proceed after a monster called the Demogorgon was summoned by Mike, acting as the party's DM. Urged by Lucas, Will, the party's wizard, casts a "fireball" attack, a move requiring a 20-sided dice roll of 13 or higher. Suspense builds as the tossed die rolls off the table. The party begins to frantically search for it so they can determine the outcome of Will's magic spell. At this pivotal moment, Mike's mom informs the group they need to finish playing as it is a school night and Mike runs upstairs to argue for more time to finish the campaign. Meanwhile, the group finds the die and determines the roll had only produced a 7, meaning Will's character would have been defeated by the Demogorgon. The friends briefly debate whether this roll should count, as Mike was not present to witness the outcome. However, as the friends are leaving Will confesses to Mike the roll had been unsuccessful. Eerily, this is the last conversation Mike and Will have before Will is dragged into the Upside Down. While all these initial moments are driven by the tabletop driven narrative, communication, problem solving, and honesty are applied well beyond the table for each of these characters.

Stranger Things and its interweaved use of D&D player characters demonstrates an alternative persona through which viewers can see each party member and their attributes from a different vantage point. The characters used in the original party are Will the Wise, a magic user played by Will, Sundar the Bold, a knight played by Lucas, and Nog, a dwarf played by Dustin. An illustration of these characters drawn by Will can be seen in Season 1.

In Season 2, we are introduced to a new character that joins the party through unconventional means, Max. Mike initially protests the addition of Max, stating their party is "full", insinuating she does not have a place in their established friend-group. In Season 2, Episode 3, Mike recounts the adventuring party's characters and classes in a way that merges their game with real life, stating, "I'm our paladin, Will's our cleric, Dustin's our bard, Lucas is our ranger, and El's our mage". It was a testimony of the already perfect party synergy of a warrior, a healer, a spell caster, a dexterous fighter and a support focused character. During this heated exchange, Max insists she can be the party's "zoomer", a class that does not exist in accordance with the rulebook.

Let's take a closer look at these D&D characters and explore how they reflect the characteristics of those playing them.

Mike, the Paladin

The 5th Edition Players Handbook describes Paladin's as holy warriors and champions of justice, describing Paladins as heavily armored knights who wield divine magic in their quest to uphold righteousness. They swear oaths that guide their actions and grant them extraordinary abilities[8].

Mike himself is often portrayed as the heart of the friend group, from his history of playing the party's DM to his tendency to maintain high moral standards. He is the first to trust Eleven, quickly adding up that something wasn't right. He encompasses a strong sense of morality and is protective of his close friends.

"R-U-N" – Will, the Cleric

Clerics are described as devout servants of deities, known for welding divine magic to heal wounds, protect allies, and smite foes. They can serve various gods and goddesses, embodying different domains of power, such as life, light, or war[9].

Will embodies this role as a shy, artistically inclined child who is protective of his friends, even as they grow older, and their relationships and interests begin to change. After he returns from the Upside Down, he remains tied to the alternate world through visions, like a Cleric receiving visions or guidance from their connections to divine realms. Through everything, Will continues to play a pivotal role in defeating the monsters of the Upside Down, despite his inherent fear from all he endured while trapped in the alternate realm.

"Flay this, you ugly piece of s***!" – Lucas, the Ranger

Rangers are skilled trackers and expert marksmen, excelling in wilderness survival. They form a deep connection with the land and often have a favored enemy, which they hunt with exceptional proficiency[10].

In Season 1, Episode 1, as Mike, Dustin, and Lucas continue their search for Will, the boys meet in Mike's basement to review supplies brought for aid in the search. While Dustin shows everyone a bag full of snacks, Lucas displays various weapons including binoculars, a knife, and a slingshot, he has brought, ready for a fight to get his friend back. Lucas very clearly expresses his disagreement with Dustin's choice of provision, arguing the importance of weapons over snacks, questioning Dustin's ability to take this task seriously.

"She will not be able to resist these pearls" – Dustin, the Bard

Bards are charismatic performers and spellcasters, using their artistic talents and magical abilities to inspire allies, hinder enemies, and shape the course of events. They are versatile characters who excel in both combat and social situations[11].

Dustin exemplifies the qualities of a real-life Bard as a charismatic friend with the ability to charm those around him into being more cooperative. An example of this is in Season 2, Episode 3 when Dustin's mom accuses Dustin of acting weird before observing a box in Dustin's hand, which unbeknownst to his mom was carrying an otherworldly creature lovingly named Dart, rattling as if something alive was inside, causing his mom concern and the family cat to hiss knowingly. Dustin deflects this by telling his mom he rigged the box with a motor to make it look like he'd caught a ghost, a quick lie tying in the shaking box as an extravagant addition to his Ghostbusters Halloween costume. His mother appears relieved and begins to chuckle and Dustin responds by laughing harder and harder to distract his mother from any further questioning before quickly leaving the room after what could only be described as an incredibly successful real-life charisma check.

"I'm the monster" - Eleven, the Mage/Magic-user

Mages, in earlier editions of D&D as the party would have been using in the 1980's, were considered magic users, described in the original basic rules as "humans who, through study and practice, have learned how to cast magic spells"[12]. The source of their power comes from their magical abilities. In later editions of D&D, mages are further defined as sorcerers, warlocks, and wizards. Eleven's personification of a mage is quite literal. Interestingly, Eleven is never portrayed participating in a D&D campaign with the others, yet she is still accepted very much as a member of the party. Eleven possesses incredible telekinetic abilities however it comes at a price, ranging from a bloody nose to physical exhaustion, and her powers are finite. Eleven spends the entirety of her young childhood at the Hawkins Lab honing her skills and her powers can be observed both growing immensely or ceasing to exist altogether throughout the seasons of the show. In Season 4, Episode 3 Mike describes Eleven as a superhero and Eleven rejects this description citing her loss of powers, declaring she is no longer a superhero without her magical abilities.

"I'm fine, okay? I mean, as fine as someone who's hurtling toward a gruesome death can be" - Max, the Zoomer

Zoomers do not exist in any Player's Handbook and would be considered a homebrew character creation; a formal depiction of the defining attributes of a zoomer is never revealed. This in itself is representative of Max's role within the friend group, as she struggles to find her place, constantly seeking stability within the group. When a homebrew character is created, it is often at the dungeon master's discretion. Fittingly, it is Mike, the party's typical Dungeon Master, that is most unwilling to allow Max into the party initially, only made more difficult by Max's choice not to abide by the classes that already existed in D&D lore.

Symbolic exploration: D&D and The Upside Down

Stranger Things offers a rich tapestry of metaphors, providing a diverse array of symbolic elements for exploration and interpretation. While this is very clear in the way D&D is portrayed throughout the show, the Upside Down provides another opportunity for this kind of symbolic exploration. Any symbolic representation of the Upside Down has never been confirmed by the show's creators, leaving viewers to draw their own conclusions. However, from a psychological perspective, the Upside Down serves as an intriguing reflective exploration into the complexities of mental health.

Childhood Trauma

The Upside Down serves as a mysterious and unsettling parallel dimension, intertwined with the real world but distinct in its nightmarish qualities. The concept of parallel realities in *Stranger Things* mirrors the duality of lived experiences, where the external appearances may not accurately reflect internal struggles. In a metaphorical representation of mental health challenges, the Upside Down offers a perspective through which to explore the intricacies behind the façade each character erects in the real world. The monstrous creatures in the Upside Down, notably the Demogorgon, Mind Flayer, and Vecna, can be seen as symbolic representations of mental health challenges. The Upside Down itself mirrors the emotional landscapes of the characters, symbolizing the parallel dimensions of reality and the profound impact that trauma can have on an individual's emotional well-being.

Will, after being abducted and trapped in the Upside Down before being rescued during season one, becomes a poignant embodiment of childhood trauma. His experiences in the alternate dimension result in an ongoing connection to Vecna, a connection to which he struggles to overcome, depicting the lingering impact of trauma on mental health. As the rest of the childhood friends continue to grow and develop into teenagers, Will remains seemingly stunted in his childish inclinations. While the other group members begin to shift their focus to navigating romantic relationships, Will desperately attempts to organize D&D sessions only to be denied by the party members in favor of maintaining their focus on the opposite sex.

Similarly, Eleven, having been subjected to unethical experiments at the Hawkins National Laboratory, demonstrates ongoing inability to discern between the very essence of what is good and bad. Her telekinetic abilities, once her only attribute seemingly worthy of love from Dr. Brenner, "Papa", becomes a weapon to be forged by her own free will. This evolution of her abilities represents both personal growth and the implication she possesses the ability to take back her own identity. Throughout, the Upside Down continues to represent a manifestation of her traumatic experiences, symbolizing the distorted reality and emotional turmoil she must navigate in a constant battle to continue growing into the person she wants to be while struggling to overcome the identity of a monster created and controlled by Dr. Brenner.

Friendship and Loyalty

A major theme threaded throughout the seasons is the resilience of human connections. Friendship is central to the storyline, shifting from a group of boys playing D&D in the basement to true camaraderie. Their shared tabletop experiences and triumphs serve as a beacon of hope as they continuously navigate the threats of the Upside Down, a metaphor for the trials and tribulations faced throughout childhood in the context of navigating new and ever-evolving relationships. Even as the friends grow, change, and move away from one another, the Upside Down remains a very central part of each of their lives.

Eleven's journey introduces an additional layer to the theme of friendship, emphasizing the concept of found family. Estranged from her biological mother, Eleven discovers a new sense of belonging with Mike, Dustin, Lucas, and eventually Will. Eleven is quickly taught the party's most valued rule: Friends don't lie. This decree becomes a pivotal anchor point for which Eleven learns to navigate relationships and the world around her. It is through friendship, something that has quickly become so vital to her core, that she first chooses to utilize her telekinesis powers as a weapon against a mutual foe, a bully that confronts the party after a school assembly.

Sacrifice also becomes a major theme, in conjunction with friendship and maintaining loyalty. The willingness of the characters to make sacrifices for the well-being of their friends becomes a poignant expression of allegiance. For example, Mike was willing to throw himself off a cliff to save Dustin from bullies. Eleven, having previously disappeared, returned in time to use her telekinesis powers to save Mike from his fall before sending the bullies running in fear.

By delving into the symbolic and metaphorical elements woven throughout the seasons of *Stranger Things,* we observe an evolving exploration of mental health themes. Once we uncover these foundational concepts, we can examine the group's D&D campaigns through a therapeutic lens to better understand their pivotal role in the characters' psychological journeys.

The Therapeutic Lens

The therapeutic lens offers a framework for understanding the psychological and emotional underpinnings of behavior and interactions. In the context of *Stranger Things*, this perspective allows us to analyze how the characters' experiences, especially through their D&D campaigns, contribute to their psychological growth, both individually and relationally.

Group Dynamics

There 11 forces that are thought to promote change in therapeutic groups[13]. Of those 11, *Stranger Things* exceptionally demonstrates two core forces, universality, defined as experiencing a sense of commonality in realizing that others share similar experiences or struggles, and group cohesiveness, defined as a sense of belonging, acceptance, and solidarity that fosters a supportive and healing environment within a therapeutic group. Throughout each season, there is a heavy focus on universality among the party after sharing the unique experience of discovering and encountering the Upside Down. As a result of the group's lived experiences in learning about this realm and their connection through the knowledge of its reality, they are often the first to believe the seemingly outlandish claims from individuals outside of their established friend group of otherwise unexplainable events at times when other community members would not be so likely. An example of this is in Season 4, Episode 2 when Eddie hesitates to recount to Dustin and friends the details of witnessing the bizarre way in which a cheerleader named Crissy died while floating in the air. Dustin and his friends reassure Eddie that they are not going to accuse Eddie of being crazy, inferring they have also experienced bizarre situations. Similarly, group cohesiveness is an ongoing theme within the party as each member, especially in the earlier days when Dustin, Lucas, Mike, and Will are four otherwise outcasted children, is provided with a sense of belonging they may not have otherwise experienced. This bond lasts throughout the duration of their adolescence and can be seen extending out to newer group members as they become part of the group.

Dr. Yalom also describes the five phases of a therapeutic group as forming (the orientation phase), storming (the transition phase), norming (the cohesiveness phase), working (the performing phase), and adjourning (the termination phase)[14]. The friends in *Stranger Things* are first introduced to viewers as a cohesive group, appearing to have much experience navigating the fantastical worlds of D&D. When looking through a therapeutic lens, this group would be considered in the norming phase as group-specific standards have presumably already been established, alliances have formed, and there are instances where current party members very expressively disapprove of newer party members. One example of this is when the group first comes across Eleven and Lucas is initially untrusting of her, resulting in several arguments before Eleven's trust is fully earned by all group members. This same scenario is apparent again when Max moves to town and Mike is not willing to include her as part of the party, citing the reason as being the party is "full", despite Eleven seemingly being gone.

Play

Psychoanalyst Erik Erikson[15] described how allowing children to play out their experiences is the greatest self-healing modality available to children, further stating that it is through play that children explore the unfamiliar and make it familiar, thus facilitating understanding of self, others, and their experiences. Play therapy pioneer Virginia Axline described play as the "child's natural medium of self-expression"[16]. The cast of *Stranger Things* use their D&D characters to do exactly this.

The core of play therapy is founded on the underlying principle that the play itself is the source of change, not the medium or the moderator by which change occurs. Exploring this concept more deeply, a play therapy approach incorporates what are described as the Therapeutic Powers of Play[17]. These core agents of change are classified within four essential categories: facilitating communication, fostering emotional wellness, enhancing social relationships, and increasing personal strengths.

The party can be observed naturally integrating many of these core agents throughout their play time, typically using D&D or video games as their preferred medium for play. The core agents of change can then be seen spilling out into their real lives as the friends begin to understand the strange events in Hawkins and prepare to take on the real-life equivalents of their roleplaying game adversaries. For example, communication, using metaphors, becomes an important learned skill. One of the first prominent instances of this is when Eleven, who had been nearly non-verbal when the group first met her, is able to utilize the party's D&D board as a form of communication to attempt to describe to the party where Will had been taken. She does this by holding up the miniature for Will The Wizard, labeling it "Will", flipping the game board upside down, and using the Demogorgon miniature to show the group what Will is hiding from. The party responds knowingly, having experienced battling the Demogorgon previously through play.

As an example of increasing personal strength through creative problem solving, in Season 1, Episode 5 Dustin relates the Upside Down to the Veil of Shadows, a formerly played D&D campaign. He can communicate this by utilizing information from his campaign binder. In the following episode, the party is determining the best course of action in locating the rift to the Upside Down when Dustin reminds the group about the Bloodstone Path. This instance in the former D&D campaign, reminds the friends of the time when the party had been split and became disabled, insisting the group should remain together in real life as this similar scenario did not pan out during play after the group chose to split their party apart.

Group Storytelling

Dungeons and Dragons is, at its heart, a fantasy group storytelling game. Using stories as a therapeutic tool can be a meaningful intervention[18]. Stories complement the overarching tenants of play therapy in that they can communicate acceptance, provide space for the expression of emotions, and enhance relationships. Likewise, storytelling allows for similar outcomes whilst encouraging additional opportunities for the exploration of areas like self-expression and creative problem solving. Group storytelling, then, has the potential to combine individual growth with the previously discussed group therapeutic forces.

Further, as a theoretical framework, group play therapy has the capacity to provide a more compelling environment with additional benefits compared to individual play[19]. This is observable when considering possible outcomes had the friends never formed a D&D party to begin with. Each party member brought something different to the table, as observed by the group members' reflected strengths, weaknesses, and personalities defined by their in-game characters. Outside of D&D, the friends have varying interests, which become increasingly more apparent as they grow older, and it's possible without the shared interest of D&D they would have experienced significantly more isolated childhoods. Group members, individually, were otherwise considered outcasts within their school peer groups, as witnessed from various bullying experiences. It was the group together, a power in numbers, that provided the space for the friends to learn life skills that may have otherwise been delayed, such as resilience, teamwork, and self-esteem.

Individual Growth

The skills learned within the core D&D group eventually can be seen translating into their individual lives outside of the party. By season 4, the party's core D&D group has physically dismantled as Will and Eleven move away from Hawkins, Lucas migrates toward varsity basketball, and Dustin and Mike join Hellfire Club. Furthermore, Eleven no longer has her powers and Will is no longer experiencing visions. Yet despite these major changes and ongoing growing pains, there are still prominent glimpses into the ways the childhood friends utilize the life skills developed earlier on.

Lucas, for example, finds himself in a position where he is forced to choose a side between his new varsity basketball friends and his childhood friends, Dustin and Mike, when Eddie is accused of the murder of Chrissy and goes missing. The varsity basketball team begins to look for Eddie, a witch hunt Lucas initially partakes in, before he begins to see that his other friends may be in danger due to their close relationship with Eddie. Lucas chooses to warn his friends, and eventually joins them in their effort to protect Eddie, representing continued group cohesiveness despite the barriers of change.

Additionally, as an example of rupture and repair, after Will and Eleven move away from Hawkins, Mike and Will's friendship begins to fade. When Mike flies out to visit, it is clear their friendship has become strained and awkward. Both former best friends initially have a difficult time seeing the others' perspective and blame each other for the lack of communication over the previous year. However, in S4E8 Will reveals a painting he has been working tirelessly on depicting the friends' D&D party and has depicted Mike's coat of arms as a heart, explaining, "that's what holds his whole party together, heart. Because without heart, I don't fall apart, even now, especially now". On a surface level, Will explains in this tearful monologue how difficult this year has been for Eleven saying, "she's so different from other people. And when you're different, sometimes you feel like a mistake", however it is apparent to the audience Will, who has arguably been struggling with his own sexual identity, is truly referring to himself in this scene. Will continues to spill his heart to Mike about how much he needs him under the guise of referring to Eleven. This was an important scene and turning point for Mike, a difficult conversation made possible by the trust and companionship built throughout childhood. This highlights the possible reasoning behind why D&D is so important to Will, as a tool allowing him to explore his values from the safe distance of his player character. This important scene with Mike brings some of that into real life as Will begins to explore acceptance of his own identity outside of the game.

Concluding Thoughts

The exploration of the therapeutic powers of Dungeons and Dragons within the context of *Stranger Things* not only delves into the early days of geek culture but also reveals a reflective metaphorical journey into the mysterious world of the Upside Down. This chapter has highlighted the therapeutic potential embedded in therapeutically applied D&D, where the collaborative storytelling and problem-solving aspects of D&D contribute to the characters' mental and emotional growth. Through the lens of their favorite fantasy game, the party in *Stranger Things* embark on more than just a fantasy adventure as they navigate the intricacies of life, facing challenges that mirror the complexities of mental health. The metaphorical explorations of the Upside Down serve as an emotional reflection of the characters' internal struggles. As the narrative unfolds, we witness not only the resilience of the friends, but also the transformative role D&D played in shaping them into strong young adults with high moral values. In essence, the therapeutic journey of the characters in *Stranger Things* is a testament to the profound impact that shared storytelling and communal play can have on personal growth and well-being.

1. Dictionary.com (n.d.). *Geek.* Dictionary.com. https://www.dictionary.com/browse/geek

2. Dictionary.com (n.d.). *Nerd.* Dictionary.com. https://www.dictionary.com/browse/nerd

3. Tocci, Jason (2009). *Geek Cultures: Media and Identity in the Digital Age.* Publicly Accessible Penn Dissertations. 953. http://repository.upenn.edu/edissertations/953

4. McCain, J., Gentile, B., & Campbell, W. K. (2015). *A Psychological Exploration of Engagement in Geek Culture. PloS one,* 10(11), e0142200. https://doi.org/10.1371/journal.pone.0142200

5. Woo B. (2012). *Alpha nerds: Cultural intermediaries in a subcultural scene.* European Journal of Cultural Studies. 15, 659-676.

6. Wizards of the Coast (n.d.). Welcome to D&D. Wizards of the coast. https://dnd.wizards.com/start-playing-dnd

7. Wizards of the Coast. (2014). *Player's Handbook* (5th ed.). Wizards of the Coast.

8. ibid

9. ibid

10. ibid

11. ibid

12. Gygax, G. & Arneson, D. (1981). *Dungeons & Dragons Fantasy Adventure Game Basic Rulebook.* Random House.

13. Yalom, I. D., & Leszcz, M. (2020). *The Theory and practice of group psychotherapy* (6th ed.). New York. Basic Books.

14. ibid

15. Erikson, E H. (1963). *Childhood and society.* New York, NY: Norton.

16. Axline, V. M. (1969). *Play therapy* (Vol. 125). Ballantine Books.

17. Schaefer, C. E. & Drewes, A. A. (2014). *The therapeutic powers of play: 20 core agents of change.* Wiley and Sons.

18. Carlson, R. & Arthur, N. (1999). *Play therapy and the Therapeutic Use of Story.* University of Calgary.

19. Sweeny, D., Baggerly, J. & Ray, D. (2014). *Group Play Therapy: A dynamic approach.* Routledge.

Chapter 4

The Marginal as Monstrous

Eleven and Will

Isobelle Whinnett

O ver the last 15 years we have seen a steady increase in the percentage of LGBTQIA+ (lesbian, gay, bisexual, transgender, intersex, queer/questioning, asexual) representation in television with the number of LGBT scripted regulars on broadcast networks increasing from 1.3% in 2006-2007[1] to 8.6% in 2023-24[2]. Notably, at the time of this writing, Netflix holds the highest number of queer characters[3]. Female characters are also fighting for equal representation on television with 45% of all speaking roles on original streaming programs being female and 44% on broadcast network programs in 2023, a decrease from the higher percentage in 2021-22[4]. These depictions of female and queer characters are attempting to move beyond one-dimensional tropes which unfortunately still exist for both. For LGBTQIA+ characters we see an association with death and trauma. For women, it is still common to see 'fridging' (the death of the female character to further the male protagonist plotline) and the trope of the 'strong female lead'.

Popular fantasy and dystopian television are pushing the boundaries to allow these characters to become more three-dimensional, no longer relying on dated homophobic and misogynistic narrative stereotypes to exist in media. This means allowing LGBTQIA+ characters healthy, flawed relationships, a backstory that does not necessitate violence or death and a plotline that can progress outside of their queerness as a focal point. It also means allowing women to exist beyond the men in the narrative, have autonomy and decision-making abilities, have complex relationships with other women and be allowed to express their identity in ways that do not always conform to traditional feminine traits.

Despite these aims, many tropes remain prevalent in our entertainment media, such as the habit of killing off queer characters as seen in Joffrey Lonmouth in *House of the Dragon* (HBO), Castiel in *Supernatural* (Warner Bros Television) and Rich from In *The Flesh* (BBC). For women, we still see many examples of harmful tropes such as the 'strong female lead' as seen with *Marvel's* Natasha Romanoff and *DC Comics'* Diana Prince. These characters conform to stereotypical constructions of character archetypes rather than being allowed the same narrative affordances of their straight conforming counterparts.

These examples highlight a process called "othering" which is a process in which a person or group are transformed by a difference they possess and stigmatised by the dominant 'in-group'[5]. Othering is often associated with monsters that are used as representations of groups with stigmatised traits such as queerness. A common example is the vampire, often used as a figure to represent the threat to social order that queer sexualities present to heterosexual and patriarchal family structures[6]. Othering is a common practice for queer characters and gender non-conforming characters in the media, particularly in young adult dystopia and fantasy. Will and Eleven are the perfect characters to showcase the attempt to move towards a more progressive protagonist but failing to avoid falling into old tropes.

The young adult dystopia and fantasy genres have historically shown growing flexibility in their presentations of women, gender non-conforming and queer characters. We see this in some examples of women from 2010's media like Katniss and Johanna Mason from

The Hunger Games (Lionsgate) and queer characters such as Klaus in The *Umbrella Academy* (Netflix) and Alec Lightwood in the *Shadowhunters* (Freeform). *Stranger Things* attempts to build on a growing trend to allow queer and women characters powerful narratives as protagonists but falls into the trap of allowing harmful tropes to creep into their characterisations.

While media has made great strides in including representation of atypical characters, in lead roles, in well-produced shows, Eleven and Will fall prey to old stereotypes and the traditional sense of "othering". While these characters are multi-faceted and three-dimensional, they ultimately reinforce the idea of the "other", linking their characters with the monstrous aspects of the story, such as death and destruction, alongside recurring themes of self-loathing, trauma, and suppressed identity. In this chapter, we will explore the characters of Eleven and Will across the span of four series of *Stranger Things* to explore how their representation links to this idea of "the other as monstrous" as they continue to fail in finding true acceptance in Hawkins.

The Other as Monstrous

Links to death can be seen in all genders whose presentation of their identity or sexuality does not conform, male gay depictions on screen are a key touchstone in discussions of the patriarchal society's dependence on gender performance. The ultimate societal transgression for a young man is to not live up to the strict measure of dictated masculinity. Where women and female characters are not meant to be so visible or powerful, the male character is stereotypically supposed to be visibly powerful, physically unbeatable and proactively interested in romantic and sexual interaction with the opposite sex. When looking at *Stranger Things*, our viewpoint character is Will Byers who is incapable of meeting these heteropatriarchal requirements for what makes a man. The narrative, perhaps unconsciously, punishes Will for these male deficiencies by having the monster abduct him and forever link him with this theme of death.

Whilst the queer and gender non-conforming characters of the eighteenth and nineteenth centuries were more openly vilified and presented as monsters, contemporary creators are less overt in presenting this connection. These gender and sexual identity character archetypes are not presented as monsters but are instead given attributes and experiences that signal to the audience that these characters are not normal, they are not like the majority. They are carefully constructed to highlight aspects of their identity that are seen as transgressive whilst simultaneously connecting their narrative to the monster, emphasising that these two things are to be seen in an equal light. To make our gay characters werewolves or our female characters witches is not enough, they must ultimately cross societal boundaries as well as fantastical ones and retain their link with the monster.

Likewise, the queer character's constant association with death and the threat of death aids in their connection with monsters. Queerness is not permitted to exist in a heteronormative and patriarchal world and so is viewed as transgressive and threatening purely for existing. Additionally, as queerness is a potentially invisible identity, it brings fears to the surface that homosexuality and queerness could exist in anyone. Queer theorists have examined the world of the socially acceptable heterosexual and the socially transgressive homosexual or queer as worlds that mutually haunt on another, each one a threat to the existence of the other[7]. The homosexual/queer world threatens the stability of heteronormative structures. The heterosexual world threatens the life and wellbeing of the queer individual. The existence of the gay/queer character as one who haunts the heterosexual society but is never allowed to 'cross over', may be one reason the queer character as a ghost or as connected to death and monsters has persisted this long. Queer characters are made to feel the weight of existing liminally, both in and on the edges of society, alive but narratively steeped in a legacy of death.

Contemporary young adult television has perpetuated this trope of the queer character associated with death/the undead in characters such as Alec Lightwood from the *Shadowhunters* (Freeform) with his hidden sexuality and the near-death experience that sparks his queer romance. *Shadow and Bone's* (Netflix) bisexual Jesper Fahey uses magic or 'small science' to move metal and make his bullets always hit their target. The *Umbrella Academy's* (Netflix) gay Klaus Hargreeves has the power to see the dead and is haunted by his dead lover in a closeted 1960's era timeline. Ambrose Spellman from the *Chilling Adventures of Sabrina* (Netflix) is a gay mortician who has the power of necromancy and is trapped, unageing for over 70 years. These appearances are not limited to male presenting characters with similar links to death present for Nico Minoru, framed for murder in *Marvel's Runaways* (Hulu), teenage vampire Juliette Fairmont in First Kill and Scylla Ramshorn, a 'necro Witch' in *Motherland* (Freeform). This connection to death mirrors the apparent border crossing outside of both the living world and the world of acceptable sexual and gender identity and presentation.

The ultimate border crossing for women under patriarchy is superior power. To give a female character limitless power is a signal that she is doomed as she has broken the natural law, is a threat to herself and has become a strange and twisted perversion of what a female character 'should be'. She should, according to these norms, be able to perform and pass as conforming to gender stereotypes to a point before this becomes out of their control[8]. This natural law of gender normativity must be narratively restored. This is shown as the 'strong female lead' breaking gender conformity rules with her extreme power and being punished, tamed and restored to her less powerful and therefore more feminine self. The heteronormative status quo must be re-established by the end of the episode.

This need to not just erase powerful and therefore gender nonconforming women but show them as powerful, losing control and then put back into their less powerful place has been repeated in Young Adult literature and in contemporary television and film over and over[9]. Both Willow and Buffy in *Buffy the Vampire Slayer*

(Mutant Enemy/Twentieth entury Fox) become too familiar with the depths of their own power and must be brought back down to Earth to avoid this descent into evil. Similar depictions are seen in *The Chilling Adventures of Sabrina* (Netflix), *Morgana from Merlin* (BBC One), *Marvel's Scarlet Witch* (Disney+), and *Charmed's* (Spelling Productions) Halliwell sisters. This narrative pattern speaks to a desire for more powerful female leads but a fear of committing to them. Their power is a threat that makes them far more frightening than the werewolf or the vampire and they must be defanged before they lose their femininity entirely. The *overly*-strong female lead acts as a cultural marker, signalling a fear and sense of threat that a limitlessly powerful woman presents and making her 'monstrous'. By portraying this as something unnatural, too transgressive and dangerous, the resulting punishment and removal of power becomes justified. It becomes a heteropatriarchal act of preservation of good rather than a systematic control of female power. We see this repeatedly with Eleven's characterisation.

The importance of 'The Upside-Down' world is also useful in this discussion as it operates as a stark visual representation of the two worlds Eleven and Will are caught between. Visual cues to let the audience know a happy heteronormative ending has not been achieved are constant. In the last episode of Season 2, Eleven attends the Snow-Ball and gains the adolescent milestones of her first school dance and her first kiss with a boy in the same night. She is dressed in feminine clothes and blends into the crowd of her peers. It would seem she has shed her transgressive self and fully assimilated. However, the camera flips, showing us that The Upside-Down still exists even here at the school dance and Eleven cannot sever this connection. Meanwhile, even though he escaped the Mind Flayer, throughout Season 3, Will senses when the monster is near as his body physically reacts with goosebumps. His own body acting as a connective tissue between him and the monster speaks to how deep the link goes. Will tries to forget his experiences and move on but his body betrays him, something he cannot override.

Traditionally, as seen in the ghost story, the monster exists liminally, both in yet not part of our world, - it inspires fear, it crosses boundaries, does not or cannot conform and challenges heteropatriarchy often with its dark allure and challenges what true reality is[10]. These characteristics are projected onto the two character archetypes. Their combination connects them to death and presents them as beings of 'excess', making them unable to fit into the confines of gender and sexual norms of society. This pins them as 'Other' with no foothold to enter or return to society. This means no matter how progressive the narrative may appear, the characters with alternative gender and sexual identities can never be afforded the same narrative freedom as a straight, gender-conforming protagonist. It is clear that *Stranger Things*, despite foregrounding the viewpoints of queer and gender non-conforming characters, cannot resist the temptation of attaching the lingering presence of death and the monstrous to these characters, marking Will and Eleven and outsiders to heteronormative culture.

Evolution of Representation: "The Other" in Media

The "other" in media has typically been used to represent groups who struggle for acceptance and are discriminated against for traits deemed undesirable or atypical. For an audience member who resonates with the other-ed character, this can cause some real harm. Studies have shown there is a link between media representation and an individual's process of self-acceptance[11]. The evolution of media representation to show traditionally other-ed groups in positive and three-dimensional narrative is crucial to removing harmful stereotypes. We will look at the evolution of representation for LGBTQIA+, gender non-conforming and female characters to show how entertainment has paved the way for Will and Eleven's arrival.

Representation of LGBTQIA+

Queer protagonists in television are becoming more common in the twenty-first century. Early appearances of queer characters were often used as punchlines or punching bags, rarely a protagonist and their story tended to be only concerned with their own queerness with critical theorists concluding that early 2000's television portraying LGBTQ characters had not progressed beyond the phase of 'ridicule'[12]. When not the butt of the joke, media turns to the opposite end of the spectrum and associates queer characters with trauma and death. The infamous 'Bury Your Gays' trope, also known as Dead Lesbian Syndrome (killing off your gay/queer character, often right before or as they consummate their queer desire) has haunted the characterisation of queer characters across various media forms. Originally appearing in media at the end of the 19th century, the trope was introduced to allow a loophole for gay authors to write gay characters without backlash due to homophobic laws at the time[13]. However, the trope continues to be used despite no longer being a necessity for queer representation with a disproportionate amount of queer women characters killed in contemporary television series[14] such as Lexa from the 100 or Maya from Pretty Little Liars. This trope perpetuates a cultural link in media between the queer character and death, encouraging a connection between the two and the ongoing acceptance of violence against queer people as something to be expected[15].

This link can be traced back in media over time, particularly in the Victorian period which used monsters as vehicles to represent threats to social order[16]. Turn of the century Victorian Gothic literature was preoccupied with the image of the monster as literary representations of members of society whose 'transgressive' identities could cause Victoria era norms to crumble. These monsters were representative of a number of marginal groups seen as transgressive including queer people, people of colour and women who did not conform to heteronormative standards. The vampire was a common way for authors to both demonise colonised lands and critique the monstrous nature of the British Empire. This has expanded with the doppelganger and the ghost, as common figures used in the representation of queer figures in media with a history of authors both attempting to derealise the queer individual and using the ghost as a means to present the half-seen reality of queer love in a heteronormative reality[17].

Representation of Gender Non-Conforming

Characters who are overtly gender non-conforming have been played as one-dimensional with male characters who do not conform to gender norms given a connotation of queerness and female characters who operate outside gender norms either vilified as freaks or lauded as one-dimensional powerhouses devoid of depth. The gender non-conforming character sticks out in a narrative that values straight, cisgendered characters and therefore is drowned in trauma to justify their existence to the viewer. As gender non-conforming characters become more common, they often fall into a new category, a cousin of 'Bury Your Gays/Dead Lesbian Syndrome' – 'The Traumatic Backstory'. These characters must have been subjected to intense violence, sexual harassment, grief and more to validate their inclusion and seeming interruption of a 'normal' story. This also continues to cement the link between queer/gender non-conforming characters and traumatic experience[18].

Monsters have also been used to represent gender non-conforming individuals. In particular, the Witch has been used as a versatile figure to show gender non-conforming women as transgressive and threatening figures as well as a means for women to express and control unspeakable desires[19]. The Witch is a symbol of potential to destroy patriarchal order and their community[20]. Rather than be permitted to push societal boundaries on the rules and expectations of gender performance, entertainment continues to reprimand characters that do not conform to strict gender norms or identify as transgender, shown within narratives such as Theo Putnam in The Chilling Adventures of Sabrina, victim to awful bullying due to not conforming to gender norms. Will and Eleven both struggle with their inability to fully perform the expected gender roles in Hawkins and are punished viciously as a result.

Representation of the Female

Contemporary television is giving more visibility to female characters, but old tropes persist. The trope of 'fridging' female characters (killing, sexually harassing or taking their power) is slowly being abandoned and the 'strong female lead' takes its place. Although the strong female lead is more powerful and present, feminist theorists have discussed the trope's tendency to view these characters as strong for their performance of masculinity and not their femininity which is viewed as weak[21]. Women in media must adhere to set rules and criteria that justify their existence. If the old criteria was to be feminine and die, the new criteria is to be masculine and fight. The tropic strings have not been cut and women must still play by the rules of acceptable femininity to deserve the role of protagonist. They must not go too far.

The 'strong female lead' presents a paradox to the media it is designed for. The strong female lead must perform masculinity to be seen as strong and further diminish their feminine traits, often through androgynous aesthetics, (dark colours, short hair, no pink, less emotion, etc.) to rid themselves of the weakness associated with femininity. However, these stereotypical and heteronormative associations with binary gender make the 'strong female lead' a complicated character to keep in check. Heteronormativity works to instil traditional gender roles. The 'strong female lead' challenges the idea that women are weak and shows them as powerful, sometimes more powerful than their male counterparts. To resolve this issue, the narrative punishes women who take their power too far, reestablishing the power dynamics and making it clear that women's power in media has strict confines. A great example of this is Jean Grey from X-Men, she is established as one of the most powerful characters in the DC universe and always takes this power too far and must be reigned in, by force. Remain within these confines and you are permitted to exist as the 'strong female lead' but break through them and the narrative will punish you, often violently.

Female characters, too, are represented through monsters to represent their straying from the social order by acquiring too much power (the witch) or leaving the heterosexual/cis-gendered brick road (the ghost/the vampire). By placing female, LGBTQIA+ and gender non-conforming characters alongside the vampire, the witch, the ghost, or in this case, the Demogorgon, you allow the Gothic tradition of linking identities viewed as transgressive to 'the monstrous' to creep into contemporary narratives. The Demogorgon, the Mind Flayer and Vecna's respective connections to Will and Eleven speak to this media trope. Furthermore, this constant appearance of monsters alongside queer and gender non-conforming characters in *Stranger Things* certainly cements the association between the two and establishes Will and Eleven's portrayal as adding to a history of these kinds of characters being represented as monstrous outsiders to heteronormative culture.

Case Study of Queer and Gender Non-Conforming Link to Monsters: Will Byers & Eleven

Will Byers

The characters of Will Byers and Eleven maintain a connection to 'The Upside Down' and the monsters within it, throughout the four seasons of *Stranger Things*. This connection is accompanied by key themes of self-loathing, trauma and suppressed identity that, when examined, shed light on how the association with monster's links to the characters' gender non-conformity and queerness.

When we meet Will, he very quickly goes missing, taken by an other-worldly force unknown to the characters and viewer alike. As Will has reached young adolescence, a point at which boys are expected to begin to progress into adolescence and adulthood and fulfil their heteronormative roles, Will disappears. As a queer character, adolescence marks a period of change which can be painful and revelatory. Will's disappearance not only speaks to a subtextual desire to deny the oncoming revelations but is a visual signal that Will cannot progress in the same way that his friends can and will forever have his path diverge from his heterosexual peers. Even when Will is still missing, adults are still discussing the question of his queerness and his bullies are still mocking his queerness as if this takes precedent over his wellbeing. When Will does return, he's called 'Zombie Boy' by the other children at his school, proving he cannot escape to a happy ending, his connection with death haunts him even after he survived and continues living. In his school and the Hawkins community he is treated with mockery and discomfort in equal measure, the school crowd parts as he walks by, and stares follow him. He also coughs up physical reminders that he is still connected to the monster and the other world. The audience is constantly reminded that Will and Hawkins are painfully aware of his status as something 'Other' and will not let him forget it.

As Will gets older, he clings to childhood and struggles to progress into the expected habits of adolescent young men such as romantic interactions with girls. He refuses to leave childhood behind, hiding in this liminal state, much as he did in Castle Byers, to avoid the terrifying truth that awaits him should he leave. The truth that he is both queer and still connected to the monster are too painful and would make him an outsider from his community so Will chooses to delay the inevitable, attempting to stay in the safe, undefined period of childhood innocence despite Will's childhood being fraught with danger but viewed in hindsight as innocent and safe[22]. Will cannot embrace who he is and exist safely and openly in his community of Hawkins. He must choose to stay a half-hidden version of himself or live authentically and be shunned from his community.

Will Byers is a young boy when Season one of *Stranger Things* begins. When we are first introduced to him, he is bullied by other boys at school. Very quickly in the first episode Will goes missing, abducted to 'The Upside Down'. Although we do not get much insight directly from Will in the first series, we do hear accounts of him from the people left in Hawkins. When his mother reports him missing she comments that Will's absent Father had called him a slur for a gay man and the Chief of police asks if it is true. Will's Mother Joyce responds, 'He's missing, is what he is!' (S1,E1). In that moment, it is deemed more important to establish if Will is queer than whether he is alive. Later in the season, his bullies mock Will's disappearance to his friends, they say Will isn't missing but rather that 'He's dead, probably murdered by some other queer' (S1, E3). The horror of a missing child presumed dead by many is not enough to banish the comments on his potential queerness. We see this again when his bullies (still mocking an absent, possibly dead boy) ask Will's friends what they have to be sad about as Will is 'in fairy land now, right? With all the other fairies. All happy and gay' (S1, E4). In a very short space of time, without Will even being present, we learn that a parent, an authority figure and Will's peers are questioning Will's sexuality and often pre-emptively shunning him for it.

The audience is signalled to that even the possibility of queerness in a child who may be dead in Hawkins must be rooted out and high-lighted. When Will is rescued from 'The Upside Down' and returns to Hawkins, he is ridiculed as 'Zombie Boy' and although he is mocked, we see a healthy amount of fear from his peers also. Will is, in effect, a revenant having returned from the dead after his own funeral. His return associates him with death, something the narrative will not let us forget as 'Zombie Boy' still cannot escape the monster in how his community treats him.

His association to death as 'Zombie Boy' does not only prompt a wave of self-loathing but is a stark reminder of the trauma he has experienced. We watch throughout Series Two as Will experiences the results of his traumatic experiences, both mentally and physically and these lines are often blurred. Will coughs up physical pieces of the monstrous 'Upside Down', he experiences flashbacks and snaps to and from 'The Upside Down' without warning and is completely alone. In a period of time where his friends are starting to notice attraction to the opposite sex, Will is ricocheting between traumatic responses and therefore cannot develop into adolescence with the same ease as his friends. The threat of death remains constant. If Will stays where he is, he must confront the monster that seeks to take him back to 'The Upside Down' and if he progresses and moves forward, he must confront the reality that he is not going to form attractions to the opposite sex as he is not straight. When discussing the feeling of the monster/Mind Flayer from 'The Upside Down' Will says 'At first, I just felt it in the back of my head. I didn't even know it was really there' (S2, E3). This could easily also relate to his experience of recognising his own queer identity. The result of the trauma from his community regarding his queerness and his body from his experiences in 'The Upside Down' is a paralysis driven by fear. Will clings to childhood, not moving forward, attempting to remain stuck in time like a ghostly version of himself whilst his friends grow up and move on. Will's trauma tangles his queer identity and his experiences with the monsters and prevents him from safely evolving as he associates both facets of himself with 'wrongness'. The monster and his queerness will prevent him from existing safely and peacefully as his authentic self in Hawkins.

As Season three progresses, it is clear that Will understands his own differences but is attempting to ignore them. He is disgusted by his brother Jonathan's romantic exploits with his girlfriend and protests when Joyce tells him he will one day feel differently, saying 'I'm not going to fall in love' (S3, E1). His certainty in this statement shows that Will has acknowledged his queerness on some level. However, he is still trying to cling to and recreate safe, untroubled scenes from his childhood. As his friends frantically discuss how to get their girlfriends back, Will desperately tries to interest them in Dungeons and Dragons, in costume and theatrics. His friends leave him to pursue their girlfriend-related issues and Will calls after them 'Guys, I'm still here!' (S3, E2). Series Three is a marked change in their friendship dynamic and Will is undoubtedly getting left behind. This is spotlighted in a grim fight between Will and Mike in which Mike argues 'It's not my fault you don't like girls' (S3, E3). Will is clearly distressed about losing Mike to his girlfriend and is seemingly half-aware that this may be due to an unrequited attachment to Mike. It returns to the subject of Will clinging to childhood with Mike saying:

> 'I'm not trying to be a jerk, okay? But we're not kids anymore. I mean, what did you think? That we were never going to get girl-friends? That we were just going to sit in my basement all day and play games for the rest of our lives?' (S3, E3)

Will is visibly distressed and replies 'Yeah, I guess I did. I really did' (S3, E3). This is a moment of painful realisation that Will's ideas and hopes for the future not only leave the safe childhood scene behind but diverge from the heteronormative futures of his friends. He cannot follow them into heterosexuality and is therefore alone, recognising his own sexuality and its consequences as a permanent marker against what is 'normal' and often considered 'preferable'[23]. Will's isolation is a key running theme to his character as well as a growing need to suppress his identity. Again, the monster and his queerness become tangled as he can make sense of neither and both place him as an outsider and in danger. *Stranger Things* utilises Will's struggles through these themes of suppressed identity, trauma and self-loathing to create media that emphasises the queer character's relationship to the monster as a marker of his exclusion from heteronormativity.

Eleven

The character of Eleven constantly finds herself in tension with her own ability to cross the border between acceptance in Hawkins and acceptance of her other-worldly power. Her power and connection to the monster directly hinders her ability to be accepted in the hetero-normative Hawkins society. When we meet Eleven, she is utterly on the fringes of society and has no feminine or cultural currency to gain entrance into Hawkins' wider society such as appearance, relationships or language. Eleven first appears already connected to the monster and with incredible power. She is a girl who has a shaved head and no markers of femininity, even being mistaken for a boy by an adult she encounters in the first episode. She has no family, no community, and appears to have escaped a hospital or mental institution, her hospital gown giving a visual cue that something is wrong. Additionally, she has limited language, hardly speaking at all in the first series. Eleven is too visible and powerful which makes her a threat to Hawkins' delicate societal norms.

As Eleven gets older and attempts to conform, forming relationships, dressing within the bounds of feminine propriety of the time period, learning better language skills, she then begins to be punished for still retaining her power. It is important to note that Adult Development theorist studies have shown that not only would young people use everyday life gender norm experiences when supporting or challenging media gender norm perceptions but they would often discuss childhood experiences when specifying gender norm expectations[24]. Childhood is a crucial time of development for concepts of gender normativity. During her childhood, Eleven's family and friends are placed in continuous danger and her family relationship with Father-figure Hopper is problematised. Eleven has more power, acting as a threat to Hopper's stereotypical stoic hypermasculinity which often fails to prevent danger befalling Eleven and others, creating a sense of shame for his masculine failures and projected anger and guilt onto Eleven for being capable of performing the protective role deemed as unsuitable for her gender. Additionally, Hopper's parental smothering provokes in Eleven the need to rebel against his parent-as-authority-figure role in true Young Adult fashion that often revolves around creating and resolving parental conflicts[25]. She loses autonomy and freedom, having to hide her powers and stay locked away. When she inevitably goes back to her power, she has her conformity stripped away. Her head is shaved again, her new fashionable clothes replaced with hospital gowns and her safe everyday life filled with monsters and life-threatening danger. The connotation is clear: Eleven's power prohibits integration into society, and she must relinquish it to find acceptance or else be deemed a monster.

Eleven's character is introduced in Series One with not even a name but only a number. She is incapable of conforming to gender norms even if she wanted to as she has been kept isolated and abused for her entire life and therefore is unaware of the expectations of gender performance that she will need to understand to survive in Hawkins. Eleven's self-loathing builds from this inability to perform femininity to societal expectations. Despite a life confined to a medical compound, Eleven recognises 'pretty' femininity when she sees it. This tells the audience that seeing beauty in traditional femininity is innate rather than a learned understanding of beauty standards. Eleven sadly comments on Nancy's idyllic pink bedroom and its trappings as 'pretty' (S1, E3). She does not know how to inhabit the concept of 'pretty' by herself. When she doesn't understand the concept of modesty and tries to change out of wet clothes in front of the boys they call her 'wrong in the head'. Their first questions are 'Where's your hair?' and her behaviour and appearance lead Lucas to comment 'She's probably a psycho' (S1, E2). Lucas' statement gives a nod to the trope of the 'hysterical female character' that despite Eleven's stoic appearance in the early series, male characters assume she must be incapable of controlling her emotions and state of being simply due to her being female. Her inability to conform dehumanises her further and she is shamed for not performing femininity as a natural instinct.

Eleven's power works in direct tension with her ability and desire to conform to gender norms. When she is first costumed in a wig and a dress, she likes her appearance but after using her powers damages this veneer, she is furious at the sight of her reflection in a lake. She cannot maintain the careful feminine appearance required to be 'pretty' and also defend herself and Hawkins. Her powers show her transgressive identity. Furthermore, her powers do not conform to what is acceptable for young women in Hawkins. She crosses boundaries such as when she throws Lucas away from Mike to protect him and Mike screams at her 'What is wrong with you?' (S1, E5). When using her powers to escape from the men attempting to capture her, she nearly dies. Eleven's connection to the monster is twofold: she released the monster/Mind Flayer as she opened the gate to 'The Upside Down' and also, she believes she is a monster for how much death is a result of her actions. Her trauma is prevented from having any outlet as she is forced to hide and suppress her identity to avoid capture, spending much of Series Two confined to a cabin to be neither seen nor heard for fear of being recognised. To stay hidden and acceptable in Hawkins, she must hide her true identity and her past. Her repeated murders make it difficult for Eleven to separate herself from the monster.

Eleven's name changes from the number eleven, to the nickname El, to Jane Hopper and keeps her identity in a state of flux. In Series Three, Eleven tries to conform, accompanying her new friend Max shopping at the mall, trying on outfits and attending sleepovers. Max may be trying to get Eleven to understand as she says that 'There's more to life than stupid boys' (S3, E2) but her activities work to initiate Eleven further into gender normativity as she looks and speaks like an acceptable young girl in Hawkins, similar to the narratives of teenage witches using their powers for makeovers, the powers still have the potential to cause harm as they seek to ingratiate themselves further into heteronormativity[26]. However, the monster will not allow her to forget her true nature. A playful use of her power to spy on boys leads her back to the monster and soon after she is physically infected by the monster. Using her power brings her closer to the monster and crosses societal boundaries. Eleven cannot conform to gender norms and use her powers. The monster does not give her a choice between them, they are constantly connected as proven by her relationship to Vecna being revealed in Series Four. As always, it is ultimately Eleven alone who must face the monster and fight, using power that exceeds what is permitted for a young woman to live in a community like Hawkins. Eleven struggles with this attachment to the monster and her own powers, even asking Mike 'What if I'm not good? What if I'm the monster?' (S4, E3). By the end of Series Four, Eleven has largely reverted to the character we met at the beginning of Series One. Her head is shaved, she is under the care/capture of men who abuse her and her power. It is no wonder she approaches and befriends other vulnerable children when she first appears, rather than adults, as the child and adult form opposites of innocence and experience that can be manipulated[27]. She is an outsider to the community that she would like to be a part of. Her overwhelming power connects her irrevocably to the monster and yet again to a history of media that shows queer and gender non-conforming characters as excluded from heteronormative society with the use of the monster.

Conclusion

Queerness and gender non-conformity have the potential to explore new and exciting narratives in contemporary television. A historical lingering trope to attach death and the figure of the monster with queer and gender non-conforming characters allows exploration of three-dimensional narratives but hinders progression beyond negative tropes. Encouraging 'strong female leads' whilst simultaneously punishing female characters for exerting 'too much' power speaks to confines on how far a female protagonist is allowed to go. Allowing queer characters to exist only in proximity to death creates a negative association that also constricts their narratives. *Stranger Things* continues a Gothic tradition of monsters as representations/markers of transgressive identities, the link of queer or gender non-conforming identities to the vampire, the werewolf, the doppelganger or the ghost is sustained in the Demagorgon. Although these monsters do sometimes permit their character counterparts such as Eleven to embody great power, the cost is heteronormative acceptance. Additionally, the rejection from heteronormative culture is viewed as the ultimate loss, worth giving up power and autonomy for. This perpetuates the idea that the queer or gender non-conforming young people should give up their powerful connection to the monstrous in favour of the safe confines of heteronormativity and not to do so is to be forever linked to death and cultural exclusion.

The resulting dangers of this link are representations of queer and gender non-conforming characters who are unable to 'win' or ultimately secure a happy ending as their straight, conforming counterparts can. We see this in the fact that Eleven must relinquish her power to find cultural acceptance, she either keeps her abilities and autonomy but lives in isolation or she suppresses her identity and forces herself into strict gender performance for acceptance. Similarly, Will stays frozen, clinging to childhood to avoid self-actualisation into a queer young adult who will forever be shunned by his community but this keeps him a ghostly, stuck-in-time version of himself that cannot escape the connection to the monster formed in his childhood. Will is paralysed between two forms of danger that mark him as a cultural outsider. *Stranger Things* creates an environment and narrative in which these characters' full selves are incapable of being allowed to exist in peace, they must choose what they value more: freedom or safety? This is then not so different from a history of characters forced to conform to heteronormativity or die, marked as monstrous and destined for death.

If Eleven was allowed to both use her powers and integrate into society in the way she would most like, and if Will Byers was permitted to expand his narrative beyond the deathly connection to the monster, then *Stranger Things* could explore narratives with far wider-scope for imaginative story-telling. However, this would force the narrative to not only change the way in which it tells the stories of its queer and gender non-conforming characters, but the heteronormative world in which they exist. And this appears to be too fantastical for the world of *Stranger Things* so far.

---

1. GLAAD, *Where We Are on TV* 2023-2024: 2006-2007 *Season.* (GLAAD, 2024), accessed June 10, 2024. https://glaad.org/publications/tvreport06/.
2. GLAAD, Where We Are on TV 2023-2024: Executive Summary. (GLAAD, 2024), accessed June 10, 2024. https://glaad.org/whereweareontv23/executive-summary/.
3. GLAAD, *Where We Are on TV* 2023-2024: *Summary of Streaming Findings.* (GLAAD, 2024), accessed June 10, 2024. https://glaad.org/whereweareontv23/summary-of-streaming-findings/.
4. SDSU, *Boxed In: Women On Screen and Behind the Scenes on Broadcast and Streaming Television in 2022-23.* (M. M. Lauzen, 2023), accessed June 14, 2024. https://womenintvfilm.sdsu.edu/research/.
5. J. F. Staszak, *International Encyclopedia of Human Geography* (The Netherlands: Elsevier, 2020) 25-31.
6. A. Haefele-Thomas, *Queer Others in Victorian Gothic: Transgressing Monstrosity* (Cardiff: University of Wales Press, 2012) 99.
7. D. Fuss, *Inside/Out* (Oxfordshire: Routledge, 1991), 2.
8. L. Jones, "Women and Abjection: Margins of Difference, Bodies of Art," *Visual Culture & Gender* 2 (2007): 62-71 https://www.vcg.emitto.net/index.php/vcg/article/view/20
9. E. Talafuse, "I Am The Monster: Self and the Monstrous Feminine in Contemporary Young Adult Literature," (Doctor of Philosophy, Texas A&M University Libraries, 2014), 128-129.
10. S. Brewster, L. Thurston, *The Routledge Handbook to the Ghost Story* (Oxfordshire: Taylor & Francis Group, 2017), intro, accessed 9 Dec, 2023, https://ebookcentral.proquest.com/lib/mmu/reader.action?docID=5148620.
11. S. C. Gormillion, T. A. Giuliano, "The Influence of Media Role Models on Gay, Lesbian, and Bisexual Identity," *Journal of Homosexuality* 58, 3 (2011): 350-354, accessed Jan 12, 2024, https://doi.org/10.1080/00918369.2011.546729
12. A. B. Raley, J. L. Lucas. Stereotype or Success? Prime-Time Television's Portrayals of Gay Male, Lesbian, and Bisexual Characters. *Journal of Homosexuality* 51, 2 (2008): 19-38, accessed Jan 7, 2024, https://doi.org/10.1300/J082v51n02_02
13. H. Hulan, "Bury Your Gays: History, Usage, and Context," *McNair Scholars*

Journal 21, 1 (2017): 17-27, accessed Jan 16, 2024, https://scholarworks.gvsu. edu/cgi/viewcontent.cgi?article=1579&context=mcnair

14. E. Waggoner, "Bury Your Gays and Social Media Fan Response: Television, LGBTQ Representation, and Communitarian Ethics," *Journal of Homosexuality* 65, 13 (2017): 1877-1891, accessed Dec 19, 2023, https://doi.org/10.1080/ 00918369.2017.1391015

15. T. Caprioglio, "Does 'Queer Narrative' Mean Trauma Narrative' on TV? Exploring Television's Traumatized Queer Identity," *Journal of Trauma & Dissociation* 22, 4 (2021): 452-464, accessed Jun 12, 2024, https://doi.org/10.1080/ 15299732.2021.1925865

16. A. Haefele-Thomas, *Queer Others in Victorian Gothic: Transgressing Monstrosity* (Cardiff: University of Wales Press, 2012) 99.

17. T. Castle, *The Apparitional Lesbian: Female Homosexuality and Modern Culture* (Columbia: Columbia University Press, 1993), 48.

18. Caprioglio, "Does 'Queer Narrative' Mean 'Trauma Narrative' on TV? Exploring Television's Traumatized Queer Identity," 452.

19. D. Purkiss, *The Witch in History*. (Oxfordshire: Routledge, 1996), 2.

20. B. Creed, *The monstrous-feminine: Film, feminism, psychoanalysis* (Oxfordshire: Routledge, 1993), 151.

21. D. Özkan, D Hardt. *Female Agencies and Subjectivities in Film and Television* (London: Palgrave Macmillan, 2020), 165-187, accessed 6 Jan, 2024, https://doi. org/10.1007/978-3-030-56100-0_10.

22. C. M. Wickens, "Codes, Silences, and Homophobia: Challenging Normative Assumptions About Gender and Sexuality in Contemporary LGBTQ Young Adult Literature," *Children's Literature in Education* 42, 2 (2011): 148-164, accessed Jan 15, 2024, DOI:10.1007/s10583-011-9129-0

23. J. W. Vare, T. L. Norton, "Understanding Gay and Lesbian Youth: Sticks, Stones, and Silence," *The Clearing House: A Journal of Educational Strategies, Issues and Ideas* 71, 6 (1998): 327-331, accessed 5 Jan, 2024, https://www.jstor.org/stable/ 30189392

24. H. Wenhold, K. Harrison, "Interviews Exploring Emerging Adults' Everyday Life Gender Norm Experiences, Media Gender Norm Perceptions, and Future Gender Norm Expectations," *Journal of Adult Development* 28, 207 (2021): 207-220, accessed Jan 16, 2024, https://doi.org/10.1007/s10804-020-09364-y.

25. R. Trites, *Disturbing the Universe: Power and Repression in Adolescent Literature* (Iowa City: University of Iowa Press, 2000), 65.

26. M. Corcoran, *Witchcraft and Adolescence in American Popular Culture: Teen Witches* (Cardiff: University of Wales Press, 2022), ch. 4, accessed Dec 4, 2023, https://ebookcentral.proquest.com/lib/mmu/detail.action?docID=7262905.

27. A. Waller, *Constructing Adolescence in Fantastic Realism* (Oxfordshire: Taylor & Francis Group, 2008), ch. 1, accessed Jan 14, 2024, https://ebookcentral. proquest.com/lib/mmu/reader.action?docID=348410.

Chapter 5

A Case Study of Eddie Munson

Moral Panics, Stereotypes and Masculinity

Anton Roberts

The character of Eddie Munson (portrayed beautifully by Joseph Quinn) was a late addition to *Stranger Things universe*, appearing only in season four of the series (at the time of writing). When we first meet Eddie, we learn he is a student of Hawkins High who has been held back for two years due to poor grades and lives with his uncle in the town's local trailer park. Regardless of his perceived lower-class status in the social hierarchy of Hawkins High (and the town more broadly), he is seemingly well-liked by his peers as a charismatic leader, 'metal head' (an enthusiast of all things heavy metal) and talented musician fronting the local heavy metal band known as the fearsome *Corroded Coffins*. Eddie is also the leader of the school's *Hellfire Club*, an extracurricular club for the playing of Dungeons and Dragons (D&D), a story telling based fantasy role playing game involving all manner of mythological creatures, probability, and multiheaded dice.

Being an enthusiast of metal music, the leader of a D&D club, and two-years-too-old to be a senior in high school, fuels a lot of misunderstandings and misperceptions about Eddie as a person. For example, *Hellfire Club* is portrayed as a sanctuary for nonconformists of all types and is criticized by the wider population of Hawkins out of fear from demon worship and satanic panic. There are also a range of stereotypes and assumptions made about Eddie's intelligence, level of threat and suspect morality because he lives with his uncle on the periphery of the community, in the town's trailer park. However, over the course of Season 4, Eddie dispels each of these assumptions. We witness Eddie's gentleness around his interactions with the school's popular cheerleader, Chrissy, the development of a loving a familial relationship with Dustin, and, eventually, his selfless act of sacrifice for the well-being of the town who stereotyped and scapegoated him in the first place.

In this chapter, we will explore the character of Eddie as a lens to discuss moral panic, stereotypes, and masculinity. As a multifaceted and nuanced character, Eddie provides a unique perspective to explore these concepts, in terms of how and why they form as well as how individual actions are nearly always counter to these kinds of broad strokes thinking. We'll see how Eddie isn't just a cleverly written bad ass character, but also provides us with a host of fascinating insights into individual and group behavior.

Mass Hysteria: Cue the Moral Panic

At its simplest, the phrase "moral panic" refers to an exaggerated societal reaction to a perceived or imagined threat. Moral panics occur, in a large part, due to media representations, that simplify, exaggerate, or distort an aspect of culture that has become 'suspect' or 'deviant' in some way. Human history is filled with examples moral panic thinking, one of the earliest being ancient Greece - famously the philosopher Socrates was accused and of corrupting the Athenian youth with his newfangled philosophical ideas[1] by questioning ones given role in society. This questioning of the dogma of the day, led to an extreme reaction by the Athenian people and he was sentenced to a gruesome death via the poison hemlock. We also have seen a long history of moral panics brought on by the development and popularization of new technologies. For example, widespread societal concerns that the increased education of women e.g development of the printing press, mightharm the 'weaker' sex through maladies like hysteria [2]. . That Elvis' hips may oversexualize a generation of women. Or, as shown in *Stranger Things*, that metal music and D&D may lead teenagers down a road of satanic worship and cultic mind control.[3]

Stranger Things is set in the 1980s, a time which was an oddly fruitful for the sheer frequency of moral panics it generated, particularly in the American context with its thriving (but highly stigmatized) countercultures. This period was seeing an increased cultural awareness of the imagined and real threat of cultic or coercive groups more generally too, such as Charles Manson or Jim Jones from the Peoples Temple[4]. The media abounded with tales of satanic worship, church burning by metal heads, youth suicides, bloody murders, and video games as gateway drugs to violence[5]. This continued far beyond the 1980s, with numerous high school shootings being 'caused' by particular forms of alternative music - as the now infamous case study of Marilyn Manson and the Columbine murders is a powerful illustration of [6]. This is the unique point in history where the Duffer brothers decide to base their fictional sci-fi narrative, with moral panics backdrop being intelligently explored throughout the series by the writers, both explicitly and implicitly.

According to the theory of moral panics there are three distinct phases [7] ; exaggeration and distortion, prediction, and symbolization. Media sources usually instigate Phase 1, by acting as an amplifying force for moral concern with the creation of the 'threat'. This usually occurs by exaggeration or distortion from media outlets or the use of emotive and unqualified sources. In *Stranger Things*, we see this initial stage being reflected in the show with members of the Hawkins basketball team actually referencing the now iconic '60 *minutes*' (1985) a documentary style television special, which directly linked a series of recent murders/suicides to their membership in D&D clubs. Or as one concerned mother commented on in the piece at the time, 'It's (D&D) not monopoly, there is no board, it is role playing, which is typically used for behavioral modification' [8]. Although such claims may appear absurd, even humorous by modern audiences, the perceived seriousness of the allegations at the time should not be understated. This is referenced in both by the town's extreme hysteria towards the *Hellfire Club*, and by Eddie himself when in his first scene he reads directly from a Newsweek article from the period that, *'The devil has come to America, that Dungeons and Dragons, at first thought to be harmless game of make believe now has both parents and psychologists concerned. Studies have linked violent behavior to the game, saying it promotes satanic worship, ritual sacrifice, sodomy, suicide, and even murder'*, referencing the spreading 'terror' the fantasy game had generated at the time (S4, E1). These individuals were no longer just children, they were sites of social violation, of public concern, to be viewed with apprehension out of a fear of what such a threat could cause to the fabric of society. In Phase 2 *prediction*, this represents the unfounded statement of a dire consequence occurring if some immediate (typically extreme) action, is not taken by the wider community. This is acted out most obviously through the way in which Jason Carver alludes to the possibility of further ritualistic murders if Eddie and the Hellfire club are not apprehended, and the 'curse' thus ended.

Phase Three is symbolization. This is where we typically see the establishment of a 'folk devil', which represents the main transgressive individual or group, that then becomes the target of stigmitisation/persecution. Typically, these are individuals that are already on the bottom of the social hierarchy e.g. a marginal sub-culture. In Eddie's season of *Stranger Things*, the moral panic of the town is curated around the apparently sinister 'Cult of Vecna'. Which in reality is actually the name of Eddie's D&D campaign, for which members of the group are blamed for the 'ritualistic murders' the befall Hawkins. The 'folk devil', then, is Eddie Munson, who is characterized as an existential risk to the integrity and values of the wider community. Jason Carver, the basketball captain who occupies a socially dominant position in the community of Hawkins, clearly denounces Eddie as the source of the fear, saying": '*And now this cult is protecting its leader, Eddie! Hiding him; allowing him to continue his rampage!* (S4, E6). The "symbolization" and labeling of Eddie as a 'folk devil' is because of his non-conformist presentation and (assumed) anarchist attitudes, which is what eventually triggers the community's hysteric response to the supernatural events happening in Hawkins that they cannot comprehend. Simply put, their norma- tive frames of reference (i.e. a small suburban Christian town of little change or real danger) does not allow for an understanding of the other worldly events taking place at Hawkins.

It is also important to note the religious connotations that underlie the representation of moral panic in *Stranger* Things such as Christian notions of good versus evil, and God versus satanism. Reli- gion often provides comfort, belonging and a moral framework for individuals during threatening or ambiguous circumstances, and these moral valuations tend to be more traditional/conservative[9]. We can see this in the religious language used by some of the characters in the show. For instance Jason Carver saying 'Do not be overcome by evil' in relation to the evil of D&D, he is drawing on bible verse to instill anger and create their obligation of 'manning the moral barri- cades' (S4, E6). To put this in a historical perspective, the towns treat- ment of the Eddie Munson has similar parallels to the Salem Witch Trials of 1692, itself another historical moral panic [10]. Akin to the communities of Salem, this literal witch hunting is not random, rarely did it apply to the wealthy, privileged or the 'pious'. When the town is confronted with the apocalyptic uncertainty of 'evil' Russians, parallel dimensions and grim demo-dogs/bats, the town choses Eddie Munson instead. There are also frequent mentions of secret pacts/convents with some malignant force or the devil himself, which Eddie is assumed to have made with such a creature. This working- class, social outcast 'drop out' and marginal individual, provides an understandable scapegoat for the community, whose absence they wouldn't miss. It's important not to miss the human need for some sense of agency in situations like this. In reality. the residents of Hawkins can do little to prevent their victimization from Vecna. Eddie's unfair punishment by the community grants the shared illusion that they can prevent this sinister calamity.

Stereotyping; Friend or Foe?

Now we can't talk about moral panics without a discussion into the weird world of stereotypes. It is worth reflecting upon here how the human brain tends to work in terms of how they interpret social cues. Humans are pattern seeking machines. To put another way, we love a pattern. This is the tendency to group events, ideas, or even people, we tend to categorize them by their perceived similarities[11]. Like many of our other internal processes, categorizing the things we encounter in the world is not necessarily part of our conscious awareness, but rather, is automatic. Stereotyping is one of the processes that we, as humans, utilize to put people into categories. It is a way for us to grasp phenomena, and apply a sense of structure and simplicity to a chaotic and complex external world [12]. Generally speaking, stereotyping is an effective mental shortcut that grants us information (albeit limited) on a recognized out-group as it allows us to apply a set of qualities or attributes from an individual or small group to a group at large.

Stereotypes are kind of like cognitive short-cuts, that allow us to make decisions quickly about an individual or a group. Now this isn't necessarily a bad thing, if we see a group of football enthusiasts walking down the street chanting in a celebratory fashion while wearing matching shirts, we could make all sorts of assumptions about that situation that we would probably be quite accurate. We could assume they like football for example, and that their team has just been victorious, but what about harder questions? Are they good people? Does their membership in this groups incline them more to violence and alcoholism? Suddenly it can become far more complicated and ethically fraught. Many stereotypes are relatively benign or lean into a positive association, such as the stereotype that "women are nurturing" or Canadians are nice. However, as stereotypes ignore the nuance and rich context of the person being categorized, they can also lead to harmful and dangerous assumptions and prejudice[13]. For example, the assumption that if you listen to metal music or lead a D&D group you are a Satan worshiper capable of murdering towns-people. When the community is making moral judgments on Eddie's character, his motives and behaviors etc they do not have access to any first-hand information/accounts on his actual characteristics. With the exception of the main heroes of the show (i.e Dustin, Max, Will, Eleven and Mike), no one that is making moral or legal deci-sions in regard to Eddie knows him in a personal sense.

Similarly, when we witness the death of Crissy, all the individ-uals in positions of power (e.g. the police) are drawing on these highly inaccurate stereotypical forms of knowledge on Eddie, to make deci-sions and predictions about his behaviors. We can see in Season 4 Episode 2, that during their investigation into the murder that his assumed qualities of being an anarchistic troublemaker and trans-gressor of the status quo mark him out. Information was thus reinter-preted through a biased lens of deviance and criminality. Whereas their first suspect Jason Carver, boyfriend of Crissy (partners are typi-cally the prime suspect in murder investigations) is quickly exoner-ated, in part because of his privileged position within the community. What this speaks to is the impact that power can have on our deci-sion-making abilities. One of the worrying things we see, both in *Stranger Things* and in our own day-to-day lives is how those in privi-leged positions tend to rely on more stereotypical information[14]. This forms the basis for much of the cognitive complacency we see in Eddie's more judgement and lack of police investigation to find other leads, or as the old adage goes *power corrupts*.

What is so great about Eddie's portrayal is that he is obviously self-aware of the town's stereotypical knowledge about him and the sub-ordinate place where he is placed in the social hierarchy as a result (i.e., being labelled a 'freak' and a drop-out despite his obvious intelligence and skill). We can see for example in his first scene with Crissy Cunningham, one of the later victims of Vecna that he refers to this implicit social system (S4, E1):

Eddie: *Hey, uh, we don't need to do this. Just give me the word and I'll walk away. Okay?*
Crissy: *It's not that. I don't want you to go. It's just... Do you ever feel like you're losing your mind?*
Eddie: *Um, you know, just... on a daily basis. I feel like I'm losing my mind right now doing a drug deal with Chrissy Cunningham, the queen of Hawkins High.*

By 'Queen of Hawkins' Eddie is commenting on the reality that his deviant and criminal status wouldn't normally permit such individuals to meet. Not only is he aware of such negative labeling, but he reflectively engages with it and somewhat resists it with his humorous criticisms of these obvious inconsistencies in his supposed identity. Part of the reason many viewers of ST found his character so compelling was the way in which he routinely inverts his assigned stereotype, displaying obvious wit, courage, and competency – aspects that discriminated groups who have been negatively stereotyped aren't usually permitted to have. Thankfully we all have the ability to resist the negative social labels that are assigned to us and Eddie is a wonderful reminder of that resistance. Before leaving our discussion of stereotypes it is important to acknowledge that while stereotypes are driven by an innate human need to simplify our social environment, they are *learned behaviors*. That is, we learn what qualities are associated with specific groups, either through individual experience or through other people. Stereotypes are also quick to form, but slow to change, with the beliefs rapidly becoming seen as a shared community understanding[15]. It is these groups definitions that form the basis for much of the inequality and prejudice we see in our society today.

Why Masculinity Matters in Understanding Eddie Munson

Moral panics, stereotypes, masculinity? You may be wondering how and/or why this is part of the discussions in relation to Eddie but it is really the thread that ties these first two discussions together.

Now gender as a concept is a lot more slippery than its intellectual sibling biological sex (although even that can get fuzzier than you would think but, I digress...) but it is just as important for understanding the human experience. Gender is not the number of chromosomes you possess or which hormones your body has been exposed to, it is the performance. The sets of practices the come to be defined culturally as masculine or feminine, with their attributes and roles.[16]. Masculine and feminine are terms that come with all sorts of social expectations in terms of the ways you are expected to identify and behave towards others. Although these ideas can feel relatively stable and innate, like they have always been that way, it's actually relative to the time, sub-culture and space you occupy[17].

In relation to Eddie, we are particularly interested in his ideas of masculinity. Masculinity is the ways (mostly) men, are expected to behave in society and evaluate themselves as men, through culturally created ideas of what a man should, and should not be..

Many of these gendered expectations can be profoundly harmful and limiting to men, particularly young men. For example, research has linked masculinity with poorer academic achievement [18]. Within working class masculinities in particular, there is routinely an assumption that you will do poorly at school, and that to demonstrate your intelligence publicly makes you a 'swat', which is something to be derided and mocked in others. We see this referenced in relation to Eddie as he is portrayed as a high school dropout, having repeated his school year many times. This is juxtaposed with his obvious abilities outside of the classroom as a talented musician and leader in his friendship group as the Dungeon Master of his D&D club, which as any self-respecting nerd will know (myself included) the game requires considerable mathematical and creative skill. However, it is only in the safety of the *Hellfire Club* that he is socially permitted to show such skills in the safety of his subculture. One of the wonderful aspects to Eddie's character is how he is more than aware of the ridiculousness of these constrictive gender scripts and seems to revel in it, "*I Think It's My Year, Henderson. I Think It's Finally My Year.*" (E9, S4). His obvious intelligence, despite his apparent academic failings, is one of the reasons he is perceived of as 'problematic' by his high school peers for he is violating the gender rules we all usually follow but rarely question.

This example highlights an important point – which is that masculinity can be "performed" in a variety of ways. With Eddie, perhaps the most obvious ways he rebukes traditional qualities associated with masculinity is in the way he dresses. Eddie's choice of dress for example is an intentional representation of not only his working-class status, but also his gender. His casual, scruffy appearance communicates to others that he is not male in the traditional or upper-class sense – he does not desire that kind of privilege, that notion of the nuclear family and the white-collar 9 to 5 that other men might. We couldn't imagine, for instance, Eddie hanging out and closing corporate deals in the New York stock exchange, while wearing a suit and tie. Eddie also exhibits several historically feminine traits, such as long hair a historically feminine trait, and one that would have been less accepted and more subversive than it is today (portrayed as it is in the period of the 1980s).

Eddie also displays more intimacy and emotion than is associated with traditional male performances. There can be many gender based attitudes and ideologies that can actually be harmful to those that embody them. The type of masculinity that Eddie powerfully displays is a good example of this, especially towards the end of the show. Now this may surprise the reader, but to give you a little context, men can actually have really poor health outcomes in all sorts of ways. We take more risks than women, are incarcerated at higher rates, are more likely to take our own lives, have poorer mental health outcomes, and have a life expectancy much lower than that of women . There is not an obvious biological reason for these stark health differences, suggesting that it may have more to do with our individual and cultural ideas, attitudes and behaviors. For example, for many men trying to display a more traditional masculinity, showing any form of intimacy or private emotion (any emotion other than anger really) is judged as more feminine behavior and, therefore, often seen as a demonstration of weakness[19]. Similarly, men from more marginal communities are often denied their gendered routes to gaining self-esteem via the more traditional forms of masculinity e.g. having a bread winner status. It tends to be these men that perform at the more extreme and problematic ends of masculinity. In my own research with men experiencing homelessness or imprisonment for example, this often means acting in extreme ways, such as acts of violence towards themselves or others, to mitigate their sense of shame[20]. In the criminal justice system, we often see how incarcerated men place greater emphasis on their physical/muscular power and their ability to 'do' violence, as a way of 'proving' their masculinity [21]. This is often performed because they are unable to carry out more socially acceptable ways of being seen as a 'successful man', in society. Eddie, like many working-class males from that period, were unable to achieve in other more conventional masculine ways, so he draws masculine value from other areas such as shredding a Metallica solo on a trailer roof, to attract demonic bats hell bent on his murder and devourment (S4, E8).

This tragic nature of some masculinities is displayed in the case of Eddie Munson. Throughout the season, Eddie is branded a coward for fleeing following Chrissy's death, rather than being given the emotional support necessary to any individual following a traumatic event. His inability to talk about his vulnerability is made clear in S4, Episode 8 as the kids of Hawkins are training for the final battle in the upside down. We see an interaction between Eddie and Dustin reflecting a higher level of friendship-based intimacy than is traditionally permitted between men, as Eddie says to *"Never Change, Dustin Henderson. Promise Me"* (S4, E8) (spoken as they embrace).

It could be argued that the inability for Eddie to effectively express his emotions and show vulnerability without fear of ridicule eventually lead to his death. Eddie experiences great humiliation and shame throughout the season which ultimately forces him to adopt other often-maladaptive (harmful) forms of behavior, that men often engage in, such as unnecessary risk taking[22]. It is possible this is why Eddie, in an attempt to demonstrate his 'worth' as a man, makes the decision to sacrifice himself for the sake of others by battling the demobats alone, facing almost certain death. This illustration is a powerful reminder of the constraints that we all feel with respect to our gender identities, and how these sets of normative expectations can come at a high price. This is confirmed in Eddie's last words, with his final concern being whether he was viewed as vulnerable or in some way weak by his peers, "I didn't run away this time, right?" (E9, S4). I wonder if you as the viewer expected this sacrifice from him as a male and granted him a form of prestige for doing so.

A Closing Thought

What I hope this chapter has demonstrated is that sociological and psychological insights are not only interesting to impress your friends with down the pub but that ideas but can be a powerful means for understanding a complex world, even when applied to a fictional tv show like *Stranger Things*. We have witnessed how Eddie became the folk devil of the Hawkings community by being a threat to the status quo and refusing to conform to the expectations of the town. Throughout the show and our critical analysis, we have seen the development of a moral panic, the dangers of stereotyping and the constraints of gendered scripts. *Stranger Things* provides a cautionary tale for the human reaction to the unknown, the incomprehensible, and of how we sense making creatures can demonstrate poor decision-making skills when information isn't readily available to explain what is occurring. It is a reminder of what can follow when our apparent sound human reasoning fails. Eddie reminds us all that we must remain critical to any label that is applied to us, regardless of the group we belong to. When the basketball coach Jason Carver talks about the apparent sacred 'values' of the Hawkins community, like in other moral panics these are never defined. Indeed, what connects stereotypes, moral panics and our ideas on gender is that they often reflect an unwritten status quo, that is rarely questioned. It is these social canaries down the coal mine that provide us with an essential driver for positive societal change (and usually at great cost to themselves).

In any society there is always going to be a perpetual tension, a dichotomy of two forces. One conservative force seeks to maintain everything as it always has been, the other slightly anarchistic, represented here wonderfully with Eddie Munson (as an example of a counterculture) seeks to challenge some of these narratives and social expectations, and create something new. Despite the ways in which he was villainized in *Stranger Things*, the real irony is that to those that know him that he is regarded as the real hero of Hawkins. The Duffer brothers did the impossible with this one, in one respect they created a typical stereotype of the metal head drop out, but on the other hand they instilled a real depth and complexity into his character. There is no other character in *Stranger Things* that had such an impact for so surprisingly little screen time. Every line of his dialogue is suffused with additional meaning and clever references that his supposed social superiors would never understand. Being self-aware of his predicament, his subordinate position in the town of Hawkins, he transgresses his applied labeling at every turn, rarely doing or saying what you would expect. As a long haired, metal loving academic myself, Eddie Munson is one comparison, one stereotype, that I can certainly live with.

———————————————————

1. Plato, & Gallop, D. (2009). *Phaedo* (Ser. Oxford world's classics). Oxford University Press.

2. Akbar, A. (2021, June 19). Pain on the page: is this the end of the hysterical, ill woman of literature? The Guardian. https://www.theguardian.com/books/2021/jun/19/pain-on-the-page-is-this-the-end-of-the-hysterical-ill-woman-of-literature

3. Laycock, J. (2015). Dangerous games : what the moral panic over role-playing games says about play, religion, and imagined worlds. University of California Press. https://doi.org/10.1525/9780520960565

4. Lalich, J. (2006). Take Back Your Life: Recovering From Cults &Abusive Relationships (3rd ed.). Bay Tree Publishing.

5. ibid

6. Petridis, A. (2017, September 21). *"Columbine destroyed my entire career":* *Marilyn Manson on the perils of being the lord of darkness.* The Guardian; The Guardian. https://www.theguardian.com/music/2017/sep/21/columbine-destroyed-my-entire-career-marilyn-manson-on-the-perils-of-being-the-lord-of-darkness

7. Cohen, S. (2011). *Folk devils and moral panics : the creation of the mods and rockers* (Ser. Routledge classics). Routledge.

8. BRMinstries. (2016). *Is Dungeon and Dragons Evil? 60 Minutes 1985 Special* [*Video*]. YouTube: https://www.youtube.com/watch?v=yShqF1YSfDs

9. VanderWeele, T. J. (2017). Religious Communities and Human Flourishing. Current Directions in Psychological Science, 26(5), 476-481. https://doi.org/10.1177/0963721417721526

10. Schiff, S. (2016). *The Witches: Salem, 1692 A History.* Little, Brown and Company

11. NHS. (2022, October 13). Stereotypes and Prejudice — Conscious Inclusion - Equality, Diversity and Inclusion - about. NSHCS. https://nshcs.hee.nhs.uk/about/equality-diversity-and-inclusion/conscious-inclusion/stereotypes-and-prejudice/

12. Hewstone, M., Glick, P. S., Esses, V. M., & Dovidio, J. F. (Eds.). (2010). *The sage handbook of prejudice, stereotyping and discrimination.* Sage Publications. Retrieved December 15, 2023, from https://d1wqtxts1xzle7.cloudfront.net/58028502/a4d91d9593ba5b9790c8159bf35004c

13. Goffman, E. (2009). Stigma: notes on the management of spoiled identity. Touchstone.

14. Weick, M. (2008) When feelings matter: Power increases reliance on subjective experiences. Doctoral Dissertation, University of Kent, Canterbury, UK.

15. Abrams, D. (2010). Processes of Prejudice: Theory, Evidence and Intervention. *Centre for the Study of Group Processes*, University of Kent. Retrieved from: https://www.equalityhumanrights.com/sites/default/files/research-report-56-processes-of-prejudice-theory-evidence-and-intervention.pdf

16. West, C., & Zimmerman, D. H. (1987). Doing Gender. *Gender and Society, 1*(2), 125–151. http://www.jstor.org/stable/189945

17. Segal, L. (1997). *Slow motion : changing masculinities, changing men.* Virago.

18. Ward, M. R. M. (2014). 'i'm a geek i am': academic achievement and the performance of a studious working-class masculinity. *Gender and Education*, 26(7), 709–725. https://doi.org/10.1080/09540253.2014.953918

19. Galtung, J. (1990). Cultural Violence. Journal of Peace Research, 27(3), 291–305. https://doi.org/10.1177/0022343390027003005

20. Fall, K. (2014). Homeless men: exploring the experience of shame. [Doctoral thesis, The University of Iowa]. Retrieved from: https://citeseerx.ist.psu.edu/document repid=rep1&type=pdf&doi=ab915b8b928bf4440b293fb157b16c1e-b3f4b007

21. Maguire, D. (2021). Male, failed, jailed : masculinities and 'revolving door' imprisonment in the uk (Ser. Palgrave studies in prisons and penology). Palgrave Macmillan. https://doi.org/10.1007/978-3-030-61059-3

22. Stergiou-Kita, M., Mansfield, E., Bezo, R., Colantonio, A., Garritano, E., Lafrance, M., Lewko, J., Mantis, S., Moody, J., Power, N., Theberge, N., Westwood, E., & Travers, K. (2015). Danger zone: men, masculinity and occupational health and safety in high risk occupations. *Safety Science*, 80, 213–220. https://doi.org/10.1016/j.ssci.2015.07.029

Chapter 6

Misfits for the Win!

A Strength Based Approach to Team Building

Neil Stafford, Psy.D. ABPP

The fear of the demogorgon is palpable as Dungeon Master Mike describes the scene to his players Dustin, Will, and Lucas. Dustin is sure, Mike denies. Lucas debates. Will is nervous. Mike is silent, and when the players begin to relax Mike slams the demogorgon down on the table. Our adventurers are faced with an overwhelming enemy. Dustin and Lucas loudly demand their compatriot Will take action. Will hesitates, waits, is indecisive, and the party suffers as Mike has the demogorgon rain death on the party. So, begins the perilous journey of the adventurers in *Stranger Things*. As we will see, the adventurers are nervous, hesitant, impulsive, confused, and unskilled in many ways. These characteristics create barriers. They make it difficult for the crew to protect themselves and find success against their enemies. Yet, we will discuss that it's not the weaknesses that matter most, but the strengths that carry the day.

Many of our favorite movies of the 1980s were based on the coming together of the misfits for the win. They rose above their shortcomings and were able to put it to the stronger antagonist characters. *E.T. the Extra-Terrestrial* (1982), *The Outsiders* (1983),

Revenge of the Nerds (1984), *Weird Science* (1985), *Breakfast Club* (1985), *The Goonies* (1985), Stand *By Me* (1986), and *Hoosiers* (1986) all bring together those who are not considered to be the first picks. They had substantial challenges to overcome, and the characters are presented early on as fundamentally flawed. Early on in each story we are led to the conclusion that they have no chance of overcoming the overwhelming odds because of their inherent weaknesses. Yet, as the story progresses, they all find a way to face and overcome the weaknesses and win in the end. What helps each of the characters in all these stories is their strengths. They each turn to what they do well instead of focusing on what makes them vulnerable.

In *Stranger Things* we see a similar story line. In the first season we are presented with characters who have flaws which are visible and routinely troublesome. The core five adventurers (Mike, Will, Lucas, Dustin and Eleven) are ostracized for their flaws at multiple points in the story. Eventually, the flaws are exploited by Vecna and put the heroes in mortal peril. As with the other stories presented, the heroes find ways to turn to their strengths for the win.

It would be easy to see that at least at the end of the first season all of them would warrant a diagnosis of posttraumatic stress disorder (PTSD) as the primary symptom of PTSD is exposure to death or a near death experience[1]. This is true for all of them. The symptoms and resulting behavior patterns of someone who suffers from PTSD are at many times dysfunctional and counterproductive to living a typical life. But when we change our perspective to a strengths based perspective (rather than a deficit based perspective) we can see how the characters are able to be resilient and thrive in spite of the trauma experiences they share. We see post traumatic growth.[2]

Post traumatic growth is when we show resilience, personal growth, and we embrace new possibilities. Two common characteristics they share are bravery and resilience. They face their fears even when dire consequences are possible. They put themselves in danger's path to protect their friends, family, and community. They are also resilient as they come together to support each other through these trauma inducing encounters. They keep their focus on the positive with an element of hope. An example of this is Eleven at the beginning of season four writing a letter to Mike as she is now in California and Mike is still in Hawkins. Eleven tells him of her adventures in California, looking forward to school, hopeful about making friends, and the positive things each member of her family are doing. She has hope, and she is focused on how she can live her life in the best possible way given the circumstances.

In this chapter we are going to explore the strengths of the characters in *Stranger Things* and discuss how it is these strengths which enable them to overcome the barriers and achieve something great together. Because when we take a strengths-based approach, the path to success clearer than if we make the weaknesses the primary focus.

A Strengths-Based Approach

In traditional medical model when we conduct an assessment on a person the focus is on weaknesses and flaws. We look for symptoms of disease. We make a diagnosis of a disorder, a fundamental problem or flaw. Then we prescribe a treatment to fix the problem. The alleviation of the flaws and problems is the goal. The same is true of psychology. We use the Diagnostic and Statistics Manual - Fifth Edition Text Revision (DSM-5-TR). The DSM 5, for short, is the proverbial bible for mental health professionals having a list of categories and specific mental health disorders. Each disorder has a list of symptoms and possible effects of the disorder. For example, attention deficit hyperactivity disorder is listed with three subtypes (Inattentive, Hyperactive-Impulsive, and Combined). It has a list of 17 possible symptoms, and three additional criteria for ADHD to be diagnosed. All the symptoms are deficit based such as "often has difficulty sustaining attention in tasks or play activities," or "often talks excessively." It is a lack of some ability or skill or doing too much of a particular behavior. The emphasis is on the negative. It can be argued that if this is the primary framework we use to look at people then we will begin to see all people as inherently flawed. We focus on their problems and weaknesses and miss their strengths and positive capabilities.

However, a weakness-based approach did not start the medical or psychological community. There is a prime human drive to focus on the painful and unwanted. We want to get rid of it because it is unpleasant. It is a short-term problem treatment instead of a long-term healthy lifestyle. This is sometimes called the negativity bias[3]. As humans, we tend to give more weight to our negative experiences, emotions, and thoughts. Researchers believe that we do this as a protective mechanism. We are more driven to avoid pain and situations that will cause pain more than seek situations that cause pleasure. It is perhaps unsurprising then that when viewing ourselves or others we tend to focus on the weaknesses and problems and how to remediate them.

However, in psychology there has been a movement to offer a different approach – a strengths-based perspective. While it is not the dominant perspective within the field it has been gaining ground against the traditional medical model. Some say the godfather of the strengths-based approach is Albert Bandura and his research in positive psychology, which is a field of psychology that focuses on highlighting a person's strengths. Psychologists using positive psychology work with clients to develop solutions instead of focusing on their problems.

A positive psychology approach provides an alternative approach to psychological assessment with the introduction of a strengths-based assessment model. Where the assessment focuses on identifying and maximizing an individual's positive attributes, talents, and capacities to foster personal development, enhance well-being, and optimize performance. By identifying and leveraging individual strengths, these assessments empower individuals to thrive, leading to increased happiness, satisfaction, and success across various life domains.[4]

The strengths-based model can be applied in diverse fields,

including organizational development, education, coaching, and clinical psychology. It can be utilized to enhance engagement, improve team dynamics, inform educational strategies, and promote mental health and well-being. The goal is to foster self-awareness, promote positive relationships, boost resilience, and provide a framework for personal and professional development. Research suggests that focusing on strengths can lead to increased life satisfaction and improved performance[5].

Misfits with Strengths

The idea of the "ragtag group of unlikely heroes" is a common theme in many of our favorite movies. The words "ragtag" and "unlikely" and "misfits" all set us up for images of weak, flawed, and heroes who are successful because of circumstance or luck. We have low expectations of our heroes in this setting. When they are successful, we have the tendency to see it as a result of luck or circumstance instead of their own skills and abilities. In fact, almost all of our heroes have strengths which are helping them succeed. Focusing on these strengths gives us a view of our heroes as succeeding because of what they bring to the situation, and not because of random luck. This happens to us in our own daily lives. We may have the tendency to see our success as a result of circumstance or luck instead of because of our strengths. Changing our perspective to look for strengths instead of focusing on weaknesses can give us a more positive and growth-oriented mindset, which we know leads to better long term outcomes.[6] We will look at several of the main characters from who were introduced in season one. We will identify their strengths and discuss examples of how these strengths were used to excel in some situations and accommodate for weaknesses in other situations. With a strengths-based focus we can come away with an optimistic and hopeful vision of what they are capable of accomplishing, and that the impending doomsday conflict coming in season five is sure to be a victory for our heroes.

Eleven

As a central protagonist we learn a lot about Eleven over the course of the four seasons. If we keep our initial perspective of the traditional psychological assessment, it is likely she would be found to exhibit traits of post-traumatic stress disorder and a reactive attachment disorder. While she has powerful abilities, Eleven is someone who has to overcome immense traumas. She is separated from her mother at birth. She is raised in an austere environment. She experiences substantial neglect. She is the victim of emotional and physical abuse. Eleven's language is underdeveloped. She presents as naïve and paranoid at the same time.

As her experiences at the Hawkins lab are revealed through flashbacks over the first four seasons one is reminded of the Wire Mother experiments in the 1950s. The Wire Mother Experiment was conducted by psychologist Harry Harlow[7]. In this experiment, infant rhesus monkeys were separated from their biological mothers and given a choice between two surrogate mothers. One surrogate was made of wire, providing food, and the other was covered in soft cloth, offering comfort. The hypothesis of many behaviorist psychologists at the time was that the baby monkey would prefer the wire mother who provided food, but Harlow observed that the monkeys preferred spending more time with the cloth mother. Comfort and emotional attachment were more or as important as food. Emotional support was as important to the baby monkey as physical support. This was like Eleven's experience. She reached out for Papa and wanted his love more than anything. She was willing to endure a lot to gain that love. There are many vulnerabilities Eleven has that are created from her early experiences. She uses her strengths to move past these vulnerabilities to achieve her goals.

We can view Eleven as traumatized and that her actions and choices are a result of these. However, we can also take a strengths-based perspective and see that Eleven has multiple strengths which help her to be resilient in the face of trauma. Eleven demonstrates resilience, courage, willingness to challenge authority, loyalty, and empathy. She knows what is right, makes a decision, and then follows through with resolve. Even if the choice is not the best, these qualities allow her to continue to make choices to move forward. She is not overwhelmed with failure. As we see through flashbacks over the seasons Eleven learns persistence and grit as a result of constant practice in the lab.

Eleven is empathetic and loyal. She has suffered neglect, deprivation, and emotional abuse in her childhood. Eleven connects with Mike, Dustin, Will, and Lucas within a short period of time after meeting them. This bond sees them through conflicts and points where despair could easily take over. For example, in the first season Eleven shows courage and the ability to challenge authority when she escapes from the lab. She resists Papa and the guards to flee the lab. She braves the elements of the forest, forages for food, confronts adults, and connects with the restaurant owner to get her needs met. She bravely trusts Mike, Dustin, and Lucas to follow them home to safety.

Eleven's emotional and personality strengths are powerful. They are as powerful as her telepathic abilities. The trauma she suffers during her upbringing at the lab, and the horrors of facing the evil of Vecna are enough to create a severe PTSD for anyone. The prime cause of PTSD is the direct experience of life-threatening events[8]. The neglect and emotional abuse of the lab would also cause severe attachment difficulties as well as psychological disorders such as Reactive Attachment Disorder (a condition where a child does not form healthy emotional bonds with their caretakers because of neglect or abuse at an early age)[9]. These psychological challenges would reasonably create enough social emotional hurdles for an individual to not be able to effectively develop prosocial relationships with most anyone. Eleven's resilience and other strengths enable her to overcome much of the trauma she experienced.

Mike Wheeler

Mike Wheeler begins the series as a middle school student. A clinical evaluation of Mike using the medical model would identify him as an outsider at school with a small group of friends. He is self-conscious and socially anxious. He is prone to struggle with self-doubt, jealousy, irritability, impulsivity, and withdrawal. These tendencies lead to conflict and difficulty with follow through. They create barriers to his success, and he has to find ways to cope with and overcome these challenges to help himself and his friends survive. This evaluation is excessively negative, and paints Mike as a weak and helpless individual requiring substantial support to make his way.

However, we can also view Mike as having several strengths which are the primary causes of his success in the course of the adventure. With a strengths-based evaluation we can see Mike stand out as a central character who displays leadership, friendship, emotional intelligence, loyalty, and has a strong sense of morality guiding his decisions. Mike has an unwavering loyalty to his friends. Several times throughout the four seasons it is Mike's loyalty to his found family which helps them maintain a group cohesion. In the first season we see him debating with Dustin about being able to have more than one best friend. It didn't matter to him when they became friends. It only matters that they are friends, and that they care about each other which creates a special bond between them. He shows a strong connection and loyalty to Eleven throughout the series even risking losing his friend Lucas in the first season as the rest of the group is determining if they can trust her.

Mike also has a strong sense of morals. He takes responsibility for his mistakes and offers apologies to his friends when he is in the wrong. He stands up for his friends in the face of immense pressure from authority figures such as his parents, school administration, and the secret government operators associated with the research lab in Hawkins. His conviction about what is right and wrong lead him to keep his focus on the priority that is his party and family in the face of personal peril.

Additionally, Mike shows a compassionate leadership style mixed with bravery and moral conviction. He makes decisions when the group is undecided. He prioritizes his friends' emotional well-being, and provides the needed pep talk to his friends when they need it most. We see him finding, taking home, and providing positive emotional support to Will when Will slips into the upside down during Halloween, instead of continuing to trick or treat with his group on the "best night of the year" in season two. This compassionate leadership also shows his emotional intelligence. All of these skills are on display when he brings Eleven into the group of friends. He is brave to engage her initially. He is brave and shows conviction when he is loyal to her as she finds ways to control her powers. He shows emotional intelligence by being sensitive to her needs for safety and compassion when they are harboring her at his home. Mike is the heart of the group. Will says to Mike, "Don't stop. You're the heart." Mike leads the group forward with his heart.

Lucas Sinclair

We come to know Lucas Sinclair as a brave adventurer through the series. Yet, if we take the traditional perspective we find Lucas to be conflicted about his role in the party and at school. He is jealous and overprotective of his friends. He reacts strongly to events, which can create conflict between him and his friends. While it is not addressed directly in the series yet, Lucas is an African American in a small, predominately white, midwestern town in the 1980s. It could be challenging to be the only minority in his group of friends, and to be one of very few at his school and in his hometown. We could chalk up his weaknesses as a result of his preteen experiences.

Yet, if we take the strengths based approach we find him to be the brave adventurer. He is strategic and decisive in his actions. Mike identifies Lucas as the Ranger of the party in season two. As described in the Dungeons and Dragons Player's Manual, a Ranger is one who is a deadly hunter with a connection to the wild. They are cunning, intelligent, and creative. They are focused, independent, and fiercely loyal[10]. Lucas is a core member of the party. He tends to be the more typically developed of the group, and in season four, uses his athletic abilities to join the more popular crowd of kids at school.

Since he is the more typically developed one of the group his strengths are more apparent. At the same time, Lucas is a black adolescent in a predominately white Midwest town in the 1980s. These circumstances alone are challenging enough. How Lucas copes and succeeds within this environment shows his several strengths. His strengths include courage, creativity, caution, and optimism. Rangers are courageous protectors. Lucas shows his courage several times throughout the series while being cautious and protective. His hesitancy to engage dangers or accept new people is out of a sense of wanting to protect his friends. He provides the viewpoint of what might be the dangers to consider when they want to charge in after finding Will or Eleven. Lucas seeks to courageously protect his friends as he rises up in the Starcourt Mall to distract the demogorgon as it nears their position in the Gap. He is optimistic as he shows in his relationship with Max over the summer when they break up and get back together several times, and he tells Mike that he can win Eleven back after she dumps him. Lucas prefers to develop plans before taking action. He urges the group to think of the possibilities and consider the dangers before heading out. He tells the group several times in different ways that patience may prove to be the best choice. Finally, we see Lucas use his courage, intelligence, and cunning to distract and foil his basketball teammates when they are intent on taking out the party.

Dustin Henderson

Dustin Henderson leaps off the screen with his bigger than life personality from the first time we see him playing Dungeons and

Dragons in Mike's basement. He is dramatic and empathetic. He encourages and pushes his party mates to take action and be brave. If we were to do a clinical evaluation of Dustin we could see him as a character with disadvantages. He lives with his single mom and their relationship seems one of equals more than parent and child. He often takes responsibility for his mother. He pushes back and is stubborn. He has a physical difference with his cleidocranial dysplasia, a physical difference where his front teeth don't arrive in a typical fashion[11]. It is a visible difference and makes him a more than likely target for bullying. We see that occur in the first season. Bullies take advantage of his differences and pick on him. With a strengths-based assessment we see that Dustin is resilient, optimistic, realistic, confident, brave, and an excellent communicator.

Dustin early on shows us his ability to clearly communicate his thoughts and feelings. He acts as a mediator between the friends in conflict. He is open about his feelings with the party and others. We see Dustin communicate openly with his mother and his teacher. He shows confidence in his communication skills as he takes the onus to call their teacher late at night on a weekend when they need information. We see he is attentive and intuitive when he provides the *My Little Pony* hypothesis to Erica in season three. He has paid attention to her words and actions. Then he takes his knowledge of pop culture, and boldly makes an interpretation about her motives and identity. During this same instance we also see how comfortable he is with his identity as a nerd. He boldly proclaims it.

Dustin is optimistic. We can see him call out for his friends over and over, hoping they respond. He does not despair when his new girlfriend doesn't initially respond to him. He has a plausible, realistic explanation, and moves forward confident that she cares for him. He is realistic at the same time. He presents facts to his party members, and then advocates for a plan that has a chance of working. Dustin's loyalty shows through when he supports his friends and stays with them regardless of the choice of the party. Dustin is the glue bringing the party members together when they would easily move apart due to their differences and difficulty with communicating. Dustin had a gift at defusing tension. We could interpret Dustin's strength of open communication as coming from his relationship with his mother. He develops this skill in a way that is effective as he works through communicating with her.

Will Byers

Will Byers is introduced in a situation where he is immediately facing evil and has a large decision to make. As the party members play in the basement Will is the wise mage faced with a choice to run or cast his spell Fireball. He hesitates, and the party suffers the consequences. We see Will thrust into this choice point. A clinical evaluation would show he hesitates and is indecisive. Will is fearful, anxious, and timid. He is a child of divorced parents. He lives with his single mother and older brother. He had been exposed to the loud arguing of his parents, and the demeaning of his father. His older brother and mother were somewhat emotionally unavailable to him as they lived in Hawkins after his father left. He and his friends are bullied at school. They're physically smaller and less athletic than some of their peers. This kind of assessment says Will is weak and vulnerable.

With a strengths-based assessment, we can agree with Mike when he identifies Will as the Cleric of the party. Will is thoughtful and empathetic in his approach. He is kind and sensitive to others. He is attentive and responsive to those who offer him advice and support. He is brave and resilient. Others know this about Will as evidenced by his mother sharing a story about Will when she is at his bedside in season one. She tells the story of Will giving his toy to a crying girl in the sandbox because she needed it more than he did. It is a consistent characteristic as exemplified by Will supporting Eleven when she is bullied at school after they move to California in season four. Will is resilient and a loyal protector of his friends. This is shown when he turns to face the mind flayer after his mother's boyfriend, Bob, gives him the advice to do so. The mind flayer takes over part of Will's mind. He is strong enough to resist the Mind Flayer as we see him communicate to Mike a warning about being used as a spy and Mike shouldn't trust Will. In season four Will's sensitivity and empathy is used to reconnect with Mike after a year's separation. He is also able to reassure Mike, and help Mike see his importance to the party.

Nancy Wheeler

Nancy Wheeler is a complicated adolescent finding herself through this story. We meet her as a sophomore in high school trying to do her best to find a way to fit in. A clinical assessment would highlight that she has the same vulnerabilities as many adolescents. She wants to be liked. She wants to fit in. She is afraid others will see her as a "nerd" for her academic success. We can find her being egocentric in the scene where her best friend Barbara expresses a desire to leave Nancy's boyfriend's home when Barbara is uncomfortable. Nancy ignores Barbara and focuses on connecting with Steve to the doom of Barbara when she is snatched by the demogorgon. Nancy's egocentric desire to be popular and liked also leads her to give into Steve's advances to have sex.

A strengths-based assessment would show that Nancy has a wealth of strengths. Nancy is intelligent, brave, curious, caring, disciplined, and attracted to doing the right thing. Nancy is intelligent as evidenced by her academic success. She is disciplined as shown by her study techniques, and her ability to focus on learning while alone with her boyfriend in her room. Nancy is curious as she enjoys journalism and discovering the truth behind stories, and she pushes forward into questionable situations to explore to find the truth. Nancy shows us how brave she is many times with her insistence on leading the group and putting herself in harm's way. Nancy cares about everyone in the group as she listens and tends to their needs before her own. Nancy evolves over the four seasons from an egocentric adolescent to a brave, disciplined, caring young adult standing at the front against Vecna.

Steve Harrington

Steve Harrington is introduced to us at the beginning of season one as somewhat of an annoying, popular, rich kid who gets away with whatever he wants. A clinical evaluation might show him as a narcissist who takes advantage of others to serve his adolescent ego needs. We find out as the series progresses that Steve has a challenging relationship with his parents and may experience emotional distance and being made to feel not good enough. Steve dismisses anyone who doesn't serve his interest. He bullies Jonathan Byers when he perceives him as trying to connect with Nancy. He turns on Nancy and bullies her when she doesn't give him her undivided attention.

A strengths-based assessment would show us the underlying positive nature of Steve that we start to see at the end of season one when Steve begins to act differently as he realizes his mistakes and works to make good on them. The strengths-based approach focuses on the whole person and the individual's assets. We are looking for what helps them be resilient and to overcome their challenges. We become aware that Steve's strengths were present the entire time. They are what help him be resilient and to grow into a leader. He is sensitive, brave, committed, and willing to sacrifice himself. He connects with Dustin and gives him guidance about taking care of himself and trying to connect with girls even if the guidance is misguided. Steve takes his duty to watch after the younger members of the party seriously. He goes along with them and puts himself in harm's way to defend them. We see Steve work with the party to directly confront Vecna's minions. We also see Steve take the plunge into the upside down in the lake in season four, to protect the other members of his party. Steve grows into another focused, caring, sensitive, and duty-bound paladin over the course of the series.

Concluding Thoughts

We have examined eight of the main characters who are introduced in the first season of Stranger Things. If a clinical psychologist were to examine the histories and current patterns of behavior for each of these characters, most likely the psychologist would develop a series of DSM-5 diagnoses for each character with a list of clinical level symptoms. As we have discussed there is a lot of evidence to support this approach with the characters.

A positive psychology and strengths-based approach orients our thinking to resilience and hope. It keeps us focused on our most important values and goals. We tap into the strengths we identify and know we have, to find ways to problem solve and thrive in our current circumstances just like our brave and resilient heroes. There is hope in our community. That is what keeps them moving forward.

---

1. American Psychiatric Association. (2013). Diagnostic and statistical manual of mental disorders (5th ed.). Washington, DC: Author.
2. Tedeschi, R. G., & Calhoun, L. G. (2004). Posttraumatic growth: Conceptual foundations and empirical evidence. Psychological Inquiry, 15(1), 1-18. https://doi.org/10.1207/s15327965pli1501_01
3. Baumeister, R. F., Bratslavsky, E., Finkenauer, C., & Vohs, K. D. (2001). Bad is stronger than good. Review of General Psychology, 5(4), 323–370. https://doi.org/10.1037/1089-2680.5.4.323
4. Seligman, M. E. P., & Csikszentmihalyi, M. (2000). Positive psychology: An introduction. In American Psychologist (Vol. 55, No. 1, pp. 5-14). American Psychological Association.
5. Govindji, R., & Linley, P. A. (2007). Strengths use, self-concordance, and well-being: Implications for strengths coaching and coaching psychologists. International Coaching Psychology Review, 2(2), 143–153.; Linley, P. A., Wood, A. M., Joseph, S., Harrington, S., & Peterson, C. (2009). Positive psychology: Past, present, and (possible) future. The Journal of Positive Psychology, 4(6), 504–520.
6. Dweck, C. S. (2006). *Mindset: The New Psychology of Success*. Random House.
7. Association of Psychological Science. (2018, July 20). Harlow's classic studies revealed the importance of maternal contact. Observer. https://www.psychologicalscience.org/publications/observer/obsonline/harlows-classic-studies-revealed-the-importance-of-maternal-contact.html

8. American Psychiatric Association. (2013). Diagnostic and statistical manual of mental disorders (5th ed.). Washington, DC: Author.
9. American Psychiatric Association. (2013). Diagnostic and statistical manual of mental disorders (5th ed.). Washington, DC: Author.
10. Wizards of the Coast. (2014). Player's Handbook (5th ed.). Dungeons & Dragons.
11. Shen, Y., Yue, H., Ying, Y., & Zhong, Y. (2020). Cleidocranial dysplasia: A case report and literature review. BMC Pediatrics, 20(1), 1–5. https://doi.org/10.1186/s12887-020-02115-4

Chapter 7

The Navigation and Performance of Guilt in Character Development

Holly Hawkes

G uilt, is a complex, moral emotion that occurs when a person beliefs or realizes (accurately or not) that they have done something to violate their own or a universal moral standard. Put another way, it is a reflection of one's actions. Guilt can manifest in various ways, such as anger, self-isolation, and self-harm. As humans, we often prefer to repress it, as guilt is closely intertwined with shame, a feeling we strive to avoid.[1]. Guilt can, however, serve a very important purpose in helping us build moral boundaries of what we will and will not accept from ourselves or others.

On-screen, guilt can be difficult to write and perform; particularly as repressed feelings can surface in ways unique to different individuals[2]. As with all repressed feelings, the time at which they bubble to the surface or impact how a person behaves will also vary. Some people become angry, some reclusive, and some even get a taste for it and get wrapped up in a cycle of negative or bad behaviour toward others or themselves. One could feel shame because of their guilt, while another could feel pride. As a writer or an actor, it is important to understand the nuance in these expressions when navigating of guilt[3].

What is particularly interesting about guilt in *Stranger Things* is that it gets us, as the audience, to question our own morals and where we place our empathy[4]. We are tested by questioning who we align ourselves with when there is a crisis, an issue in a romantic relationship or a friendship and, upon reflection, deciding whether we sit comfortably with a character's decision. For example, many of us were challenged at the introduction of Vecna when he made the characters face their own morality, giving the audience an insight to the character's guilt that we may not have seen before, such as with Max and Billy.

In the following pages, we will explore how the actors on the show perform guilt in Stranger Things and, specifically, how Vecna impacted how the characters navigate their guilt later in the series. We will delve into a selection of story arcs and unpack each actor's performance looking their expression and navigation of guilt[5].

Character Development: Performance and Navigation

Stranger Things has complex characters and relationships, and the development of these characters can be seen over time through their performance and how the character navigates feelings and (lack of) expressions of guilt. In this context, "performance" refers to the actor's portrayal of the characters and how a character may perform a particular emotion or act. For example, we will address Mrs Wheeler's regret after a near-guilty act and Max's apparent guilt surrounding Billy's death. "Navigation" refers to the character's journey and the tools they use to traverse various situations or feelings. Navigation Is often contextual and complex, such as Max's repression of guilt and her journey as Vecna's victim.

The development of the characters throughout the Stranger Things series is a testament to the Duffer brothers' writing skills, ad hoc writing approach, and collaboration with the actors, a common discussion in the Netflix series Beyond Stranger Things[6]. While this collaboration is not unique in screenwriting, working with young characters and actors allows for the current life experience of the young people to be implemented into the similarly aged characters. Alongside this, the age of the actors aids the development as many of the actors naturally mature and age over the series, which brings a unique aspect to the notion of navigation and performance compared to the more experienced and adult actors. For example, an actor could question why their character is responding in a certain way to a situation and perform their scene in their own way to aid the character's navigation in a way that may seem more appropriate for their age and experience, which is where performance and navigation can meet and inform one another.

Generally, the navigation of guilty acts and emotions are dealt with differently depending on the age of the characters; for the younger characters, it tends to impact their smaller social group with some exceptions, such as Will and El; these are discussed further on. Whereas the guilt harboured by adults tends to create a wider impact and ripples into other areas upon other characters, for example, Hopper navigates his guilt regarding his daughter's death while caring for El. Consequently, this has a detrimental impact on their relationship. Similarly, Mrs Wheeler almost jeopardises her family unit for Billy Hargrove and navigates her guilt differently from that of Hopper; they have different ways of dealing with this guilt, and the series explores this to great lengths.

However, in order to feel guilt, one must first establish their standards for right and wrong. *Stranger Things* does this from the very beginning. The whole series starts with the premise of simple trust between friends, a group of boys who religiously play Dungeons and Dragons in the same location and play by strict rules, and this is tested as Will, Mike, Dustin, and Lucas adopt Eleven or more that Mike forces El (Eleven) upon the group, and she is taken into their safe space, the first breach of trust by Mike which is often taken out on El by the rest of the group as she is treated like an alien (did anyone else think El was an alien in the beginning?). "Friends don't lie" is a recurring theme for the group, and it becomes their moral code, particularly for Mike and Eleven. This theme is tested to its limits and ultimately abandoned towards the end of season four as greater things are at stake. The simple and innocent basis of "friends don't lie" is an important marker in the series to help the audience understand the values and the growth of the young characters, and with lying comes the notion of harbouring secrets and guilt. Setting a code such as this creates boundaries, and should someone step over the line, they must decide whether to lie for self-gain or to protect someone or face their actions to soothe their guilt. A key example of this dilemma is El's lie to Mike about her school experience, which ends in her assaulting Angela, which is discussed further in El's section below.

Mrs. Wheeler and Billy

Karen Wheeler is a glamorous mother and wife in an emotionally and seemingly physically lacking relationship. She has money and adoring children, but Mr Wheeler is portrayed as being psychologically absent while being physically present. This is a typical 1980s family trope where gender stereotypes were still as they were in the 1950s and 60s, where family traditions seem to have frozen. The significant social and political changes over these decades created huge shifts in family life as women could work more, although not expected to, and the growth of sci-fi and other forms of popular culture was considered demonic. Everything is changing around Mrs Wheeler, and while her husband sleeps, unbeknownst to her, her eldest two children are saving the world. She is left with Holly, the youngest, and she is bored.

Billy is barely acquainted with the town before he moves on Mrs Wheeler, and they plan an affair in season three. There is a seemingly innocent build-up to this as a group of Hawkins mums regularly take the time to relax by the communal pool to watch Billy start his lifeguard shift. However, Billy takes a liking to Mrs Wheeler, and we believe this affair will happen; the Hawkins' mums seem to take a distant fancy to Billy, but there is a physical distance between them and Billy, which is shown through the camera angles. However, Mrs Wheeler breaks the boundaries of this physical distance while she and Billy privately chat about their hook-up. Billy is still a teenager, and Karen would be around her forties. The only thing that makes this bearable is that actor Carla Buono is young and glamorous, and Dacre Montgomery looks much older than his 16–19-year-old character. It feels as though the Duffer brothers are treading the line of acceptability in this era while paying homage to common relationships on screen of a time gone by, such as in *The Graduate* [7]or *Thelma & Louise*.[8] If this situation were replicated off-screen, it would certainly be problematic. So, not only are physical on-screen boundaries being broken in this relationship, but also boundaries of social acceptability, which keep the audience in check and get them to weigh up where their morals may lie.

Despite their plans, Karen doesn't turn up for the meeting; while the audience watches Mrs Wheeler reflect on her decision, we are also privy to what Billy is experiencing, and the scene from both sides is genuinely suspenseful. We can see Mrs Wheeler navigating her feelings and decision through her looks of concern at her family as she gets ready to leave for the hook-up, and Carla Buono performs her emotional journey in detail, showing the highs and the lows of her guilt but also her excitement at the opportunity laid out before her. While her decision to not go may imply guilt concerning her family, she still apologises to Billy for not turning up, which is an interesting response. She approaches the apology as a mature teenager, and it is momentarily difficult to see the age gap between the characters. Still, it shows her maturity and search for closure; she attempts to make amends to a somewhat absent Billy and return to her normal life[9]. Still, it leaves us wondering what the conversation would have been if

Billy had been the "real" Billy after the accident and not the pawn of the Upside Down with superhuman strength. Mrs Wheeler experiences a type of transformation through this navigation as she was able to weigh up the importance of an affair against her family, and her navigation of her guilt surrounding this in a way creates a positive change arc[10], but what makes the situation somewhat sad, is that she ends up back in the same situation she was in before and no happier.

Will Byers

Will Byers could be considered a protected character throughout the series; we draw up a boundary as he has a horrific first series, and the raw emotion performed on the screen allows us to accept him as a fragile human with a strong and unwanted connection to the Upside Down. We see him as having a function and as a vessel rather than being part of the friendship group, which puts him on par with El; this character link then becomes strained in season four as Mike and El have a relationship and El becomes more of a human character rather than a tool, motivating Will to be more a part of the group again. Noah Schnapp performs this brilliantly, and we see a stark contrast in his performance and navigation of emotion in season four compared to earlier seasons.

Will shows symptoms of trauma, someone who wants to hang on to their childhood and expresses his guilt as anger, isolation and frustration, which is a typical sign of regression and a lack of emotional intelligence. We can see how frustrating this is for those around him, particularly Mrs Byers and Jonathan who try to get him to communicate his experiences. This could be a complex mechanism to tell the audience that Will knows that he is different to the others and that he has lost time in his life that the others haven't, bar El. Will is put in a situation like characters such as Frodo Baggins, Harry Potter, and other world-saving people; he navigates issues where he has been dropped into a situation he did not ask for, while others are fighting on his side but often without him. This gradually becomes more serious as the nemeses get bigger and stronger, and people lose their lives.

Will doesn't seem to learn or grow, which distances him further from his friends and family, and the audience can see his battle with this. For Will, his navigation of guilt differs from those of other characters as he doesn't always get the option to explore the guilt, where it is placed, and gain any closure as the Upside Down and its inhabitants repeatedly assault him. His growth as a person is stunted, and he is constantly traumatised throughout the series, creating a form of anti-arc.

It is unsettling that he repeatedly hides signs of the Upside-Down interfering with their world and does not mention anything until another problem appears. It is often unclear whether he sees the significance of this information, but at times, as a viewer, his withholding of such information feels like a betrayal. For viewers, this is frustrating but perhaps a necessary tool to keep us on the edge as Will allows us to glimpse into his mind and anticipate what might happen without the other characters knowing. Will does have the ability and the opportunities to give information regarding his important visions and experiences that nobody else has, but he repeatedly refuses to share the information, most seen in the visuals of his neck tingles. The audience and Will know that these are significant; it is a tool in place to tell us that something bad is happening or is about to happen, but we also know that it is an important piece of information that Will often chooses to withhold. As the series reaches season four, Will develops as he is forced to be with his friendship group, and they travel larger distances to solve pieces of the puzzle. There is still a clear distance between him and those around him, and we are directed to what the fandom feels is a significant clue: his Creel-style drawing. Is this another secret that Will is harbouring?

Jonathan Byers

Jonathan Byers is another seemingly naïve character, and he is shown to understand boundaries. We go through a journey of trust with him, at first questioning his intentions with Nancy, the quiet kid with the camera, using his camera secretly around the pool party, an uncomfortable few scenes because it feels inappropriate, but then our boundaries shift, and we side with him as Steve breaks his camera and we grow to trust him as he helps Nancy after her drunken outburst at Steve and keeps her safe in her state. The character's performance is aided by Charlie Heaton's awkwardness, and it takes a while to warm up to the character and trust him. Jonathan is also steadfast in his self-belief, which opposes other people-pleasing characters like Steve and Nancy, particularly in the earlier seasons, and offers a different type of hero. This awkwardness portrayed through a character is often synonymous with guilt or potential guilt and suspicion, a tool often used to misguide the audience, akin to Severus Snape or Edward Scissorhands, maintaining a "school loser" stereotype.

During the intensity of season four, Jonathan offers a reprieve from the chaos as he is guilty of not telling Nancy about his college decisions as if this is the biggest event in the world, and he is distressed by this. Until this point, he often suffers the burden of being a kind and honest person, a stereotype of the eldest in a caring, single-parent household. Jonathan's guilt coincides with the upheaval of the family moving to a different state, where he transforms into another stereotype, that of the bong-loving teenager. This plotline feels wedged into the story, but again, this could be another mechanism to show the limits of the character; he does not become dangerous or family-destroying, but it feels like the right amount of rebellion that Jonathan is capable of. In real life, this would be a subtle change in a teenager's life, perhaps even expected; however, what we see of Jonathan in previous seasons tells us that this is an extreme transition for his character as he is ultimately naive. As there is a large amount of screen time dedicated to Jonathan and Nancy together, this offers the opportunity to see the contrast between the two; their relationship and differences show Nancy's recklessness and guilt more than the subdued and arguably level-headed Jonathan.

Anyone who experienced the isolation at school that Jonathan did would know that his meeting Argyle was a happy moment as they formed a bond. Argyle plays a significant role in Jonathan's transition in season four and his understanding and navigation of his relationship with Nancy and guilt as he openly uses Argyle as a sounding board for his college dilemma while he is guilty of lying and withholding information from someone he loves; we feel a kind of empathy for him as he tries to find a resolution. This shows a positive development in his story and relationship arc but remains to be confirmed until season five, as Steve starts making his move again at the end of season four.

Steve Harrington

Steve starts the series as an irredeemable character, suffering the pressure of being a young man in his teens, which we see again in Billy when he arrives on the scene as they almost reflect one another. At first, we get glimpses at Steve questioning his own behaviour; this is shown through the performance and camera angles of the looks he gives other characters, checking in on his behaviour and how they receive it, showing that at this time, his main concern is how others see him, which can be linked to priorities of masculinity of the era. We often see Steve at his worst when he is with Nancy, favouring sex above anything else, highlighted by sneaking into Nancy's room to distract her from her studies, despite studying being something that she feels is important and something that she is good at. Then he challenges Jonathan to a fight and the tricky matter of leaving drunk Nancy at a party, which we know is dangerous, but we are also troubled by Nancy at the end of their relationship over her drunken break-up with Steve.

Until this point, Steve appears to be an invincible bad boy who can get what he wants, but this is suddenly shattered. This is a pivotal point; we see changes in both Nancy and Steve, together and as individuals. However, for Steve, this is the catalyst that made him one of the most popular characters in the series. Over time, we see Steve transform in his duties of responsibility as a friend, a nod to Freud's notion of moving from the wanting Id and accepting the Ego to gain a balanced personality and focus on his morals[11]. He becomes a surrogate parent figure to many of the younger characters and a more honest and mature young man. His responsibility to the younger characters, particularly Dustin, holds him accountable for his actions, and his decision-making is clearly shown on screen.

There is no clear evidence of Steve ever feeling particularly guilty; he states the obvious and generally addresses problems as they arise, which would ultimately address notions of guilt before they set into more negative actions that require more navigation; he no longer isolates himself, he is less angry as he develops and becomes more apologetic, so Joe Keery's performance of Steve could be how he avoids any deep-set feelings of guilt and this could be linked to how Steve escapes the initial wrath of Vecna.

Vecna's Impact on the Navigation of Guilt

The series upholds as well as challenges sci-fi and horror tropes that we are familiar with, and one that can be seen, particularly in season four, is that coming-of-age and guilty teenagers are the first to be targeted by the villain, reminiscent of Freddy Krueger character. Analysing Vecna's victims, considering the theme of guilt, creates some interesting questions regarding his targets. The writers interestingly introduce new characters who account for some of Vecna's first victims of his most terrible punishment yet, while Max, as a main character, is targeted first; he fails initially; this makes her fate at the end of season four even more upsetting. Vecna's position is that of a type of Freudian Id vigilante, taking it into his own hands to punish and solve the issue of guilt and repressed feelings[12].

Chrissy, Wake Up.

As there were a handful of new characters introduced to develop the Hawkins world and the Vecna storyline, Chrissy is an important character to discuss. Chrissy goes along with the American Dream as a cheerleader and girlfriend to a basketball player, and they would typically be the type to get married and have great jobs; it is surprising that there was never an appearance of a promise ring. But Chrissy approaches Eddie to buy drugs because she is having headaches and visions, and she does this shortly after Max sees Chrissy being sick in the toilets. This was never fully explored in the series; rather than seeing guilt through Chrissy, we see previous trauma inflicted by her mother. However, Chrissy never seems to feel guilty, and we don't get the screen time to find out what is happening with her. She is not shown to feel guilty about attempting to buy drugs and seems rather to enjoy her experience with Eddie before her grisly death. So perhaps she was feeling guilty about something else that could have destroyed the precious American Dream, a spot of morning sickness, perhaps? It is frustrating that Chrissy is portrayed and performed as a significant character in her short screen time; she is the first to show the audience Eddie's true nature, albeit complex, and their interaction also places Eddie in the historical context of Hawkins. While they are both new characters on screen, they are not to Hawkins, and there is a history regardless of the lack of on-screen exploration. But it is unlikely that Chrissy would have been targeted by Vecna so quickly if she felt a pang of guilt about buying drugs; it almost feels like she was brutally killed without reason. However, her character placement plays a vital role in our understanding of Vecna as his killing her provides us with an example of what he is capable of and, potentially, why he does it; this sets a precedent for his future attacks and provides some context for what Max has been experiencing.

Eleven

Throughout the series, the audience is forced to fluctuate between trusting Eleven and being suspicious of her as she starts the series like a child with seemingly basic needs who struggles to verbalise her emotions and experiences. While we acknowledge that something terrible has happened to her, and she could be linked to the troubles experienced by Hawkins, she is portrayed as a regressed young girl with trauma. The series shows numerous instances where El leaves her friends for their safety, another common struggle seen in film and TV where the character wants to rectify their guilt and involvement of others, which can again be seen in The Lord of the Rings and the Harry Potter universe.

While El often persists as a socially awkward and emotional young person, in season four, while in California, she does what many guilt-ridden young people suffering from ill mental health do and expresses a new identity, although to little success, similar to Buffy Summers and Ann storyline in Buffy the Vampire Slayer[13]. She understandably goes through what is a late coming of age, following a regressed pathway like that of Will's, and lies her way through school, but most importantly, she lies to Mike about her experience, which results in her physically assaulting Angela after she persistently bullies El. This small window in time shows El as a hurt, despicable young girl with no regret or sense of guilt. While El is angry at the loss of her powers, in season four, episode two, "Vecna's Curse", she resorts to extreme violence not just by physical contact but by assessing and understanding the impact of her chosen weapon of assault[14]. It raises questions about what she would have done to Angela if she did have her powers. The performance between Millie Bobby Brown and Elodie Grace Orkin works as they are both young female actresses, and they get to act out a trope of a popular high school bully and the strange kid, but the navigation of El's guilt and anger in this episode is what shows El as a potential danger even without her powers and with a new identity.

Finally, there is the friendship between Max and El. El experiences a lot of jealousy when Max enters the scene. El has an underdeveloped understanding of human interaction and friendship, and Max is accepted far more easily by Lucas than El ever was. Like many young female friendships, it is unpredictable, and they quickly bond after a short period of animosity. Max helps El navigate her pain and misunderstanding of boys and is arguably a bad influence on her development. But with Max, we see El experiencing life as a normal girl; their friendship offers a great deal to El's development and life experience, making the finale in season four even more painful to process.

The link between former Vecna, One and El is shown in detail as a precursor to this and El is shown to be somewhat responsible for One's progression into the person he has become, and this is the guilt she is shown to hold on to, but we wait for a painfully long time for El to overcome this as she watches Max dying from the Upside Down while she lies in Lucas' arms in real Hawkins. The audience is led to believe that El, in her anguish and guilt, has a kind of regenerative power that brings Max back from death, and finally, we are left with El trying to explore Max's mind only to see that there is nothing there. It could be argued that El has a flat story arc; as much as she tries, she is too influenced by what goes on around her and her influencing it for her character to actually change.

Max Mayfield and Billy Hargrove

Max and Billy are introduced as suspicious characters; we know nothing about them, which puts our understanding in line with the other characters, and as the characters learn, we learn. There is already a secret, as we quickly understand that they have moved away from California for a reason that never comes to light. Max is portrayed as a naive character at first, at the mercy of Billy, and this is temporarily troubled after Billy asks, "Who's fault is that?" they had to move to Hawkins in season two, episode two and under her breath, she says, "Yours."[15]. This leaves curiosity and confusion when the Mind Flayer kills Billy, as the audience has unanswered questions about the Hargrove/Mayfield family. What we do know is that Max and Billy have a militant father who calls Billy a "faggot" for the way he looks at and after himself, and this has been theorised by the fandom that perhaps Billy was caught by Max with another male while back home, this could also explain Billy's obsession with Steve Harrington. The queer-to-guilt/shame relationship is another trope often shown in much queer literature and in nostalgic and pastiche television and cinema; this can be seen in films such as I Love You Phillip Morris[16] and Dallas Buyers Club[17]. It is an upsetting encounter between Billy and his father for the audience, even though Billy is horrendous to Max to a surprising degree, violating many stepsibling rivalry tropes.

He has no qualms regarding inciting affairs with married women, and he is performed as a man and not necessarily a young man until we see him with his father. Then, we see him as a young man navigating masculinity and perhaps sexuality in the late 1980s. Billy only gets to redeem himself through what appears to be him sacrificing himself at the end of season three, but does this redeem him or prove that he is guilty? Considering Vecna targets guilty characters and those with ill mental health in the later series, it could be hypothesised that even if Billy didn't crash his car and become infected by the Mind Flayer, he might still have ended up as a Vecna victim and that his demise was inevitable one way or another. It is with this that Vecna chooses to torment Max while she understandably meets with the school counsellor to help her heal and understand her mental health.

In season four, Max is portrayed as a typical, insular teenager with mental health issues who pushes her friends away while she is forced to live in a trailer with her mum, the very same trailer park that Eddie Munson lives in. Vecna's torture of Max is challenging as she appears guilty about witnessing Billy die (seemingly, for her), but Vecna claims that she was, in fact, happy for him to die. This is agitating for the audience as it would be particularly cold, especially for Max, to feel that way despite their relationship, and with this, season four ends on a question of Max's morality and the understanding of her guilt on trial. The fandom has highlighted an interesting easter egg in the aforementioned season two episode regarding Max and Billy being "stuck" in Hawkins. Are their respective endings coincidence or prophecy?

Nancy Wheeler and Barb(ara)

Nancy Wheeler traverses the different modes of young womanhood; she is intelligent, wants to be popular, and learns to break the rules. She is caring, practical, and organised in apocalypse-style activities but arguably one of the most frustrating characters to watch. The Nancy and Steve plot plays a significant role in the audience's fluctuating opinion of both characters. Steve helps Nancy be seen as an innocent, Sandy-style character from Grease[18]. Steve is initially the heartthrob of the series until we see his behaviour towards Jonathan and Nancy doing the bare minimum to challenge Steve's behaviour. Suddenly, we are torn and question Nancy's morals. We are privy to the challenges in the relationship and know that Nancy had a choice that night by the pool, Barb's death creates a divide and troubles the audience's perception of Nancy to the point where we blame her. In the scenes where Nancy and Steve go to the bedroom, it is evident that she feels guilty even before Barb is attacked. We see this through her concerned looks and camera shots towards the pool and the window from which the pool can be seen, but again, she does nothing to change the situation. This guilt is readdressed when Vecna comes on the scene in season four, and this scenario is used as his weapon against Nancy.

But why is Barb's death so significant? This could certainly be up for debate, but Barb, alongside Jonathan, are not only social outcasts like many other characters, but they are shown to feel alone; Stranger Things brings together an audience of people who have felt the same, which has aided its success on Netflix and at conventions. While Eddie is meant to champion the outcast revolution, he is not alone, like Jonathan and Barb. Barb's death is a shocking reminder of the loneliness of outsiders, those who don't go to parties to hook up, don't favour drinking and are the designated drivers. Her death feels like a betrayal to the fans; therefore, while she was a minor character on screen, her impact can be found throughout many series episodes, including in later seasons where Nancy tries to investigate the death further, perhaps to ease her feelings of guilt at what could be considered the bargaining stage of guilt.

Throughout the series, Nancy does show guilt, but only because they are keeping the secret about Barb in relation to the Upside Down. However, this is often linked to Nancy's visions of herself with Steve in the bedroom as Barb sits alone, and Nancy breaks every promise that was made to Barb, and there is perhaps an element of shame linked to sex, too. The performance of Nancy's guilt is somewhat "textbook" as she goes through anger, depression, and bargaining and, in the end, tries to accept the situation, which does show that she transitions, develops and navigates guilt, growing as a young woman and forms a positive change arc.

Conclusion

The small range of characters set out in this chapter shows how complex the notion of guilt can be navigated on screen through characters by the performance of the actors, the writing of the script by the writers and their collaboration with the cast. Large chapters could be written on single characters alone, such as El and Hopper, who traverse a variety of feelings and the expanse of their consciences almost episodically, but analysing other support to main characters can highlight just how important it is to show the complexity of emotions and conscience in those characters too. This can allow more depth to the Stranger Things world and a realistic portrayal of everyday people from a time gone by in an unrealistic situation. This is important because it means that the series doesn't need to lean on world-ending monsters and travesties to carry it; it is our care, understanding and support for the characters and their relationships that the audience is invested in.

There is a stark contrast between the characters who navigate guilt alone, like Hopper, or readily face it like Steve, and those who fall under Vecna's curse, like Max, El, and others, as he forms the vessel for people facing their demons (figuratively and somewhat literally) and guilt; this has formed a complex development in the plot as the seasons develop, once again showing the skill of the cast and crew.

---

1. Shave, D. W. (1974). Depression as a Manifestation of Unconscious Guilt. *Journal of the American Academy of Psychoanalysis*, 2(4), 309–327. https://doi.org/10.1521/jaap.1.1974.2.4.309

2. Christopher. (2023, November 23). *How To Describe Guilt In Writing [17 Best Tips + Examples] - Writing Beginner*. Writing Beginner. https://www.writingbeginner.com/how-to-describe-guilt-in-writing/

3. Glicksman, E. (2019, September 12). *Your Brain on Guilt and Shame*. Www.brainfacts.org. https://www.brainfacts.org/thinking-sensing-and-behaving/emotions-stress-and-anxiety/2019/your-brain-on-guilt-and-shame-091219

4. Gaut, B. (2010). Empathy and identification in cinema. *Midwest Studies in Philosophy*, 34(1), 136-157.

5. Chamarette, J. (2012). *Phenomenology and the future of film: Rethinking subjectivity beyond French cinema*. Palgrave Macmillan.

6. Dempsey, M. (2017). *Beyond Stranger Things*. Netflix.

7. Nichols, M. (Director). (1967). *The Graduate*. United Artists.

8. Scott, R. (Director). (1991). *Thelma & Louise*. MGM Pathé Communications.

9. Donovan, B. (2022, October 24). *Character Arc Generator (50 Types of Character Arcs!)*. BRYN DONOVAN. https://www.bryndonovan.com/2022/10/24/character-arc-generator-50-types-of-character-arcs/

10. First Draft Pro. (n.d.). *4 types of character arcs*. Www.firstdraftpro.com. Retrieved June 1, 2024, from https://www.firstdraftpro.com/blog/four-types-of-character-arcs#:~:text=Character%20arcs%20are%20crucial%20to

11. Freud, S. (1923). *The ego and the id*. Dover Publications Inc.

12. Westerink, H. (2009). *A dark trace : Sigmund Freud on the sense of guilt*. Leuven University Press.
13. Whedon, J. (1998). *Buffy The Vampire Slayer* (Series 3, Episode 1). The WB.
14. Duffer, M., & Duffer, R. (2022). *Stranger Things: Season Four* (No. 2). Netflix.
15. Duffer, M., & Duffer, R. (2016). *Stranger Things: Season Two* (No. 2). Netflix.
16. Requa, J., & Ficarra, G. (Directors). (2009). *I Love You Phillip Morris*. Europacorp.
17. Vallée, J.-M. (Director). (2013). *Dallas Buyers Club*. Focus Features.
18. Kleiser, R. (Director). (1978). *Grease*. Paramount Pictures.

Chapter 8

Trauma and Young Adulthood
Why was Billy the Perfect Mind Flayer
Chloe Stollery

S*tranger Things* as a series contains an abundance of human versus monster rivalries. Will and the Mind Flayer. Hopper and the Demogorgon. Max and Vecna. What these creatures all have in common is that they are supernatural, allowing audiences a level of distance from having to understand the emotional complexity of those in conflict with the protagonists.

However, the story is a bit more complicated when we talk about the human monsters.

Billy is introduced to the audience during Season Two as a human antagonist, presented as the bullying, erratic and abusive older brother of Max Mayfield. While he may seem like the classic "older brother bully" character, in seasons two and three we gain insight into Billy's early life, such as emotional hardship and maltreatment he experienced in his formative years at the hand of his father. These glimpses into Billy's background lead the audience along a journey of understanding and empathy, and, for many, helped to reframe the initial, negative impressions developed of him into something more positive. Less of a monster, we start to see Billy as a three-dimensional, flawed but charming character. One who woos the suburban Mom's, cares for his sister, Max, and has regrets and remorse around past decisions. Billy is contradictory, and often-times, unpredictable. In this chapter, we are going to explore Billy as a representation of trauma, and the complexity of his behaviour presentation, where surface behaviour may be driven by deeper rooted learning resulting from his past experiences.

However, before we dive into the analysis of Billy's behaviour, we first need to discuss Billy himself.

Billy Hargrove

Billy is manipulative and erratic yet has an obvious charm about him. When he first arrives in Hawkins, he quickly acquires the title of the new 'top dog' of Hawkins High School. He forms this impression, beating Steve Harrington, a popular protagonist, in the social hier-archy of best-looking, best drinker and better basketball player. As a mullet-wielding, shirtless lifeguard, he charms the generations of Hawkin's, placed in a position to pursue illicit relations with Nancy's mom, and uninhibited by humiliating others, because, hey, he's Billy Hargrove. *'Hey lardass! No running on my watch!'*.

At first glance, he seems awful. Mean to his sister, wooing suburban moms, but then over time we learn that Billy is just a product of his environment. Whilst it is easy to assume someone is mean and awful because they are just a bad person, there are usually life events that lead a person to think and feel the way that they do.

In Season 3, we learn that Billy's father was emotionally and physically abusive towards both his mother and him (S3, E8). Within flashbacks of Billy's childhood, the audience observes his intimidating nature, where he shows mistrust and uses threats against Billy's mother (S3, E6). This scene is portrayed as a storm within Billy's mind. His father is angry, he punches his wife, he uses profane language. Young Billy, unable to cope with this interaction, demon-strates distress and desperation to protect his mother by physically intervening with his father (S3, E6).

Billy's father is shown to consistently employ threats and intimidation in his interactions with Billy, portraying an unpredictable and erratic primary caregiver. During Season Three, the audience witness some of Billy's early life experiences as Eleven intrudes into his consciousness. Through this lens the audience observe Billy's anxiety and reactions to mistreatment of his mother by the hands of his father. We see these behaviours – exerting control through manipulation and the use of intimidation tactics and at times physical abuse - mirrored by Billy in his interactions with his younger sister, Max. He regularly uses intimidation towards her, using his voice and physical strength to show dominance and overpower her. We see just how much fear and control he has over her in their discussion about why they moved to Hawkins in the first place, *'Who's fault is it?... say it... SAY IT!'* (S2, E2).

This mirroring of behaviour is unsurprising considering that humans are largely social learners. Social Learning Theory is a foundational theory in psychology that explains how children learn through observation and behaviours are a product of the environment in which they live[1]. This is why, for instance, children see others clapping, they will start clapping too even if they are not sure why they are clapping in the first place. Similarly, Billy witnessed his father mistreat women in his household, and therefore, Billy too is mirroring this behaviour. As audience members, we understand Billy's behaviour to be wrong, but as we can understand where it is coming from. While audiences were initially driven to form the impression that Billy is an awful person, we slowly start to realize that is a product of his social environment and upbringing. He mirrors the misplaced anger of his father.

Whilst the behaviour of Billy towards his sister can at times appear, contradictory, it is possible that these actions are more a reflection of his inner self than the environment in which he learned. In glimpses of his early life, we see the physical altercations he has with his father arise from his protection of his mother (S3, E6). This suggests that Billy's natural character may be more that of a "protector". However, over time it has come to largely be masked by a thick armour of resentment bitterness gained from his tumultuous upbringing. It is common for trauma-experienced children to develop these patterns of behaviour in young adulthood[2]. This may be why we often see Billy is berating and taunting Max, we also see him behave in traditional, healthy ways of a typical big brother, such as taking responsibility for driving her to and from school and the arcade (S2, E1), expressing interest in her friendships and relationships, and searching for her when she's missing (S2, E9).

The Role of Trauma

There is no doubt that Billy has experienced various forms of trauma. In this context, trauma is being used to describe the experience of and exposure to a deeply distressing event[3]. Traumatic events may consist of abusive behaviour from others, be that of an emotional and neglectful nature, but are ultimately characterised by the activation of the bodily stress response, and an overwhelming inability to handle the stressors present. Traumatic events are shown to have profound effects on the development of young people, due to the vulnerability of their developing bodies and brains[4]. When such events are experienced, the brain develops alternative coping mechanisms to handle the level of 'toxic stress', and switches from development to survival mode, resulting in developmental differences in behaviour for years to come. With individuals who are trauma-experienced, there are often negative outcomes associated with prosocial behaviour and relationships with others[5]. We may theorise some of Billy's observable behaviours to be an outcome of the alluded to trauma he experienced at the hand of his father, namely his lack of empathy, emotional regulation, and social isolation.

It is important to note that this chapter may, in parts. talk in absolutes, referring to Billy's 'trauma' and other challenges he faces with his social and emotional health. As we are dealing with fiction, these absolutes can be considered perspectives to provoke an area of discussion around the morality of the character. When it comes to Billy's interactions with others, the audience are witness to some incidents and others are alluded to, which requires an interpretation to link Billy's behaviour to his experience. The chapter attempts to provide a framework where the pieces of the puzzle can be fit together but should not be treated as diagnostic but rather is meant to offer a perspective for discussion.

Billy and The Mind Flayer

In Season 3, we are introduced to the Mind Flayer. The Mind Flayer is the manifestation of Vecna's power, providing a physical form through which Vecna can control, influence, and ultimately dominate his victims towards his own ends. Over time, it is revealed that Vecna chooses his victims based on their vulnerability, able to feed on their experiences. Vecna, and consequently The Mind Flayer, obtain their strength through the trauma that their victims have experienced. In this way only those individuals who are already engaged in a battle against their own mental demons are selected, aligning perfectly with the condition of the character we are introduced to, one whose interactions comprise predominantly of bullying, use of force and control.

However, it is not only Billy's trauma that makes him susceptible to The Mind Flayer. A key driver for his 'Flayed' character is to recruit more vulnerable individuals to the bidding of The Mind Flayer. The survival mechanisms he has developed as a young person, namely his independence and ability to emotionally manipulate make for an adolescent with a keen ability to charm those around him. He goes mostly unnoticed in the form of Flayed Billy, and able to recruit others to the cause of the Mind Flayer, as well as remaining a consistent feeder for The Mind Flayer who preys upon his vulnerabilities.

Billy is complex, and we can reflect on his behaviours to understand they are a result of his experiences. Importantly, we must

119

understand exactly *how* these experiences have such a profound impact upon his behaviour.

The Origins of Billy's Troubled Nature

When Billy joins the show in Season 2, we understand this to be due to relocation of his family, including half-sister, Max. Billy makes an immediate impression at Hawkins High School; he is unhappy about the forced relocation and upheaval. His attitude towards Hawkins is dismissive, appearing to blame Max for this inconvenience and treats her with disdain (S2, E2). When delving into the depth of Billy's mind, a memory observed by Eleven shows Billy's previous closeness with his mother. When out surfing, a much younger Billy rushes to his mother to exclaim his surfing success, comfortable, knowing positive affirmation would be forthcoming (S3, E5). With the absence of his mother in the present day, and emotional response when these memories are prompted, it is clear Billy is dealing with a sense of abandonment and rejection from his mother, which is the likely cause of the rift in his attachment to his new family. As this change happens during adolescence, a key developmental period[6], we can assume this change contributes to the clear resentment he portrays towards his family and those connected to Hawkins.

Billy has experienced several adverse childhood experiences (ACE), including emotional abuse, and domestic violence, driven by father causing the change in his home and circumstance, and the loss of a safe primary caregiver, his mother. An accumulation of ACEs means Young Billy is at greater risk of later life problems, specifically relating to outcomes with his mental health and formation of positive healthy relationships[7]. His experiences are directly linked to difficulties he has in demonstrating empathy towards others, as well as a lack of inhibition towards extreme or erratic behaviour, which can be associated with difficulties he has with emotional regulation. These outcomes are observably cyclic and can also contribute towards his social isolation. Therefore, the higher the number of risk factors, the more likely are the implications for behavioural development.

Empathy: 'Bonus points if I hit 'em in one go!'

Billy demonstrates a significant lack of empathy through his interactions with those around him. He has an arguably 'toxic' relationship with Max, mirrored in behaviour he has towards others who are subjectively perceived to be 'weaker' than him. Those who are mostly vulnerable to this behaviour are Max's friends, and peers of a similar age to him.

This behaviour is observed when Billy responds to seeing Max interacting with Lucas Sinclair. He highlights his displeasure about the developing friendship, observing a tension between the two that he was uncomfortable with. He grabs Max and tells her not to talk to Lucas again, blatantly dismissing the emotional impact on Max, placing her in a position of forced surrender or deceit (S2, E4). She feels continued anxiety and paranoia at his potential response should he find out about her continued friendship with him, to which Billy is unaffected. He appears to thrive on others feeling intimidated, or even scared of him.

The focus of his behaviour is observably driven by a need to control through intimidation. His communication towards others is uninhibited by presenting disproportionate force in how he talks to them, and his physicality towards them.

Atypical demonstrations of empathy can indicate many developmental conditions. With Billy, we see he has not formed an emotionally safe or healthy relationship with his father. Attachment theory[8] posits that where early attachments, built upon emotional warmth and safety, are not formed, this can have negative long-term implications on social development, with poor outcomes in abilities to relate to others. Billy's father represents the role of an unpredictable caregiver, in stark contrast with his mother with whom he has a secure attachment. When his mother leaves him and his father takes charge of raising Billy, this triggers the behavioural changes seen in Billy in the series. We see glimpses of Billy beating other students at school, using abusive language towards them (S3, E6). He represents a product of the misplaced anger of his father, further explaining the lack of empathy we see in his blatant intimidation towards others.

Billy, however, can demonstrate empathetic behaviour towards specific characters in the show. During Season Three, when Eleven ventures into his consciousness, we see glimpses of Billy's distress around how his father treats his mother. Billy even physically intervenes between his parents' violent interactions (S3, E6), demonstrating his protective nature. This is a relationship we do not see him share with any other individuals in the show, certainly not his father with which the relationship is built upon fear, intimidation, and physical abuse; a subsequent outward projection of Billy's unhappiness. The bond shared with his mother represents his 'happiness' and the secure grounding that brought him out of the clutches of The Mind Flayer in the Season 3 finale.

Billy, as a young child, demonstrates a strong relationship with his mother creating a secure attachment. The severing of this attachment when she finally left Billy's father was likely a significant contributor to the change in Billy's presentation. His mother represented comfort and security, without which he is fearful and mistrusting. His behaviour presentation as a teenager has developed to form an armour and to mask these insecurities, meaning his treatment of others is driven by a need to protect his own emotional vulnerability.

Social Isolation: 'You shouldn't have looked for me.'

From a social standpoint, the audience sees Billy surrounded by people throughout Season Two. When introduced to Steve Harrington, a one-sided rivalry transpires, driven by Billy, leading him to feel the need to best Steve at any social activity. Billy's dominating and bullying behaviour support him to securely feel stronger than, or in control of, others within different social scenarios, such as through physical ability or social standing. In the context of these scenarios, the behaviours socially enhance Billy's reputation, portraying a character who is observably popular and admired.

As Season Three progresses, the audience observe the change in his character presentation, beginning as the buff lifeguard, swooned upon by the women at the pool, creating illicit plans of 'private swimming lessons' for Nancy's mom (S3, E1), only to be immediately taken by The Mind Flayer and forced to do its bidding. Billy succumbs more and more to the clutches of The Mind Flayer as the season develops, with behavioural changes observed by the audience but not necessarily recognised by many of the characters within the show. Nancy's mom has an entire conversation with Billy to explain why she didn't attend her 'private swimming lesson', without being alarmed enough to highlight a difference in his character whilst his mind is infiltrated by The Mind Flayer (S3, E2).

The lack of recognition of his changing condition is highly relevant considering Billy's relationships with others. His lack of interest in forming reciprocal relationships correlates with his likely developed attachment style from the severing of the relationship with his mother. A child's attachment to their primary caregiver can present itself in numerous styles, although each child's attachment is unique to their experience, environment and to an extent their genetics, it remains possible to group attachment styles based on common characteristics and traits. Some psychologists state that typical human development is characterised by the occurrence of key experiences to ensure the growth of resilience and emotional regulation[9]. If key developmental milestones are disrupted, there can be long-term implications on social development. Attachment theory suggests that when emotional safety and security are not met, child become independent of caregivers due to a need for self-soothing [10]. In this scenario, the child's developing brain shifts from a focus on growth and development, to survival – producing various behavioural adaptations and coping mechanisms which, whilst acutely beneficial, become maladaptive in the long-term. In such cases, individuals display difficulty trusting, and consequently emotional proximity may be challenging making the formation of healthy relationships with others difficult[11].

Changes to Billy's personality are obvious to the audience; his interactions with others become alien, sometimes being polite and controlled (S3, E3), and at others erratic, confused, and angry. He stops working out, participating in sports, or attending parties. He becomes insular, and disappears, but there are few individuals who pay attention to this stark behavioural change. This contrasts the way people wrapped around Will Buyers during his possession in Season Two. Whilst Will had his friends and family to provide support and protection of this external threat (S2, E3), Billy was isolated, unable to turn to a parental caregiver, isolated from his peers in a new town and unable to form meaningful attachments. Despite his portrayal as a popular individual, the superficial nature of high school popularity isolated Billy.

Emotional Regulation: '...you know what happens when you disobey me. I break things.'

The portrayal of Billy's unpredictability is reflective of his ability to emotionally regulate. The audience witnesses how contradicting his external behaviours as an adult can be from the behaviour that he displays in memories as a child.

During early episodes of Season Two, when the audience is forming an impression of Billy, scenes demonstrate just how quickly his behaviour can escalate. For example, in one scene, after picking Max up from school, Billy begins a conversation about his dislike of Hawkins. Billy begins with under the breath dismissive comments, which develops into raised voices and aggression. When Billy is within these heightened states of emotional arousal, his behaviour is erratic and unpredictable; the cool, calm, and collected manipulator is lost. His behaviour escalates to a level of uninhibited and extreme risk, and in this context, attempting to run over Max's friends (S2, E2). Billy begins a game of chicken with Max, driving at high speed towards her new friends, displaying a disregard for their well-being and the consequences of his actions. Billy shows that he thrives when instilling fear into others. He appears in a state of ecstatic euphoria when driving towards Max's friends. Coupled with dangerous driving and loud music, Billy's bodily sensory systems play into his erratic behaviour. To make sense of Billy's response to this, understanding how quickly his behaviour can escalate out of an optimal state, can provide context to his disproportionate responses.

As humans we have different levels of tolerance reflecting where we remain in a state of comfort. For every person this will be individualised, and reflective of their experiences, genetic makeup, and upbringing[12]. It is possible for those tolerance levels to be impacted by experience. The *Window of Tolerance* theory describes these tolerance levels as a spectrum, which can help us visualise behaviours experienced in a state of comfort and those within states of under and over emotional arousal[13]. For individuals who have experienced emotional trauma, the theory suggests this will have an impact upon their 'Window of Tolerance', and that they will subsequently spend more time out of their state of 'optimal' arousal, or their 'comfort zone'.

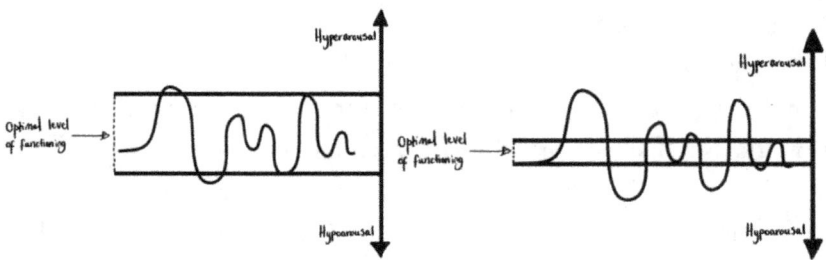

Figure 1. (left) Window of tolerance non-trauma experienced and (right) trauma experienced.

This theory explains why Billy's behaviour often appears escalatory, erratic, and misaligned with the appropriate context of a situation. Billy's behaviour demonstrates that he moves quickly through different states of emotional arousal. The audience observes Billy's most euphoric and erratic behaviour when he is in highly dysregulating sensory circumstances, including the car chase with Max, and when he is punched by Steve (S2, E8). To describe the specific emotions of Billy, it may be inappropriate to consider him 'unhappy' as a character, for he demonstrates symptoms of more positive adrenaline-fuelled emotions, such as excitement. These contexts do not prompt a rational connection between emotion and circumstance. It is highly inappropriate for Billy to be laughing hysterically when he is being punched by Steve, or when driving straight towards a road collision with Max's friends. What this does show however, is that Billy is not operating within optimal states of emotional arousal, and what appears to be true of these described behaviours is that he spends large portions of his time in a state of emotional dysregulation.

Childhood Adversity, Trauma and Charm

The scenes discussed lead to the assumption that Billy experienced high levels of childhood adversity, which impacted upon his social and emotional development in adolescence. By the end of Season Three, the audience are able to reframe Billy's behaviour as a consequence of his experienced trauma, however, for the characters within the show, no-one is witness to the context of Billy's behaviour other than Eleven. Therefore, the context for the other characters, that supports us to feel empathy for Billy, is missing.

This poses the argument of just how important understanding context is. What becomes clear about Billy's character is that The Mind Flayer has an especially strong grip on him, which is concurrent with the extent to which his trauma – namely his relationship with his father, estrangement from his mother, the physical and domestic violence he has experienced – has impacted his functioning.

As the audience are taken on the journey to understand Billy, the tone of his character shifts, from one who is imposing, strong and controlling, to a character in which the audience see vulnerability, fear, and sadness. The presentation of Billy's trauma within the show is integral in the lead up to Billy's "arc of redemption", whereby Eleven infiltrates the possession of his mind through resurfacing a memory of him surfing on the beach with the support of his mother, as a happy child with the love and consistency of a primary caregiver (S3, E5).

Moral complexity surrounds Billy, especially around how we link his behaviour to his actions. Billy bears the hallmarks of someone whose experiences have had a profound effect on their social development, causing implications for his social interactions and creating a character who the audience, initially, love to hate. This is what makes Billy such an interesting character study. The audience is simultaneously presented with someone where the focus and commentary can be on their cruel behaviour towards others, whilst being forced to acknowledge the context of his emotional development which has led him to such behaviour.

The tonal development of Billy changes as the seasons progress. Initially, the lens predominantly focuses on his behaviour, without too much background context, prompting the audience to arrange their opinions on his morality based on these observations. Yet as we are provided with more context, our perceptions potentially develop around his moral compass, his empathy, and his overall 'redemption' as a character.

His 'redemption' is triggered by the human connection made by Eleven, demonstrating her understanding of his happiness and connecting with him on a human level. This introduces a theme of his character being misunderstood, with the focus shifting from his treatment of others to how he has developed in such a way, placing the focus and lens now on his 'internal' functioning rather than his 'external' behaviour. Billy needs the audience to understand his behaviour as 'mask' or human 'armour' of his deeply rooted inner battles. Without this context, his character retains a surface portrayal of someone who is cruel and a bully for no reason.

The artistic representation of Billy's trauma as a storm (S3, E6) is consistent with the experience of a young person who is trauma-experienced and built upon the concept of unprocessed memories causing behavioural issues in later life[14]. For Billy's heroics to save Eleven and her friends at the end of Season Three, it takes Eleven to retrieve one of these memories to remind him of his core character. Billy becomes lost in the storm of his mind when he is infiltrated by The Mind Flayer, a representation of struggles with his mental health, and something we know that The Mind Flayer feeds upon.

When comparing Billy to other characters whose minds were vulnerable to or infiltrated by The Mind Flayer, Billy appeared to have a more difficult time shifting the possession that this took on his life. In Season Three, his possession was instantaneous, and he immediately begins the role of leader, working towards the desired outcomes for The Mind Flayer. In Season Two the audience sees the possession of Will Buyers to The Mind Flayer, and a fluctuating struggle to remain himself. The audience sees a significantly harder battle in Billy's mind in the limited number of glimpses we see of Billy as himself, and not possessed. This is representative of The Mind Flayer's need to feed off and corrupt those engaged in a harder battle against their inner daemons. This could contribute to our feelings around the hardship he experienced growing up, increasing our empathy for his character.

Billy's portrayal of the 'bad boy' of Hawkins, his cruel, intimidating manner to the main characters presented him as an ideal human antagonist for the show. Once the audience has gained a context for the cruel behaviour, the lasting impression that is left is one leaning towards empathy and understanding. It leaves the audience with an emotional dilemma, as we know from context that Billy hasn't 'changed', he is supported to find the core of good that exists within him, deep down underneath the trauma that drives his external experience of the world.

Concluding Thoughts

Through Billy the audience is provided with an interesting character who generates a certain degree of cognitive dissonance throughout his 'on screen life'. Billy Hargrove may not be all that he seems. There may be further context to consider when assessing motives of behaviour. Billy's initial introduction highlights behaviours typically labelled as 'toxic'; the maltreatment of his younger sibling, the competitive dynamic with Steve and the manipulation of those around him. These behaviours initially appear to have little motivation behind them other than serving to massage Billy's ego, to make himself feel powerful, or assert his dominance – in short Billy is portrayed as a one-dimensional bully. However, as the audience learns more about his character and experiences, a sense of sympathy develops.

Billy, as a teenager, is observably unable to form healthy relationships built upon foundations of trust or emotional safety. His emotional relationships exist on a surface level and do not demonstrate emotional warmth or depth. He manipulates others through control, for reasons around emotional protection and an embedded pattern of behaviour response to social learning from his caregivers. Ultimately, Billy's inability to consistently show empathy creates further emotional distance from his family and peers, leading increasingly to a place of significant social isolation, and creating a natural antagonist that slips effortlessly to the bidding of The Mind Flayer. The audience comprehends Billy's past and present suffering. The reason behind his behaviour becomes clear and the audience understands Billy is not a bad person *per se*, he's simply hurt. His antagonistic nature combined with the emotional fragility of his character create the perfect conditions for possession by The Mind Flayer, whilst ensuring the audience are left with a lasting impression of someone whose behaviour may be understood through exposure of their experience.

Many trauma-experienced individuals do not have the opportunity to explain themselves through two seasons of a show. External behaviour may not align with internal feelings, and action can be a poor method of communication of an individuals' innermost difficulties. If behaviour is communication, it can provide a lens into the context of an individuals' life. The lens on Billy's characters allows us to reflect on the presentation of trauma through an individual's behaviour and the immediacy in which we may judge behaviour, where there may be more to understand than what is presented on the surface. Regardless of what subjective lasting sentiments may be on Billy Hargrove, these opinions are importantly developed through a deeper, empathetic reflection on his experience, not solely the behaviour he presents.

Societally, we are vulnerable to remaining hyper-focused upon judging what we see without considering the complexity of the drivers for behaviour. Billy's character journey represents what is needed for trauma-experienced individuals – empathy, patience, and a willingness to deepen our analysis of what is driving surface behaviour.

---

1. Bandura, A. (1977). Social learning theory. Englewood Cliffs, NJ: Prentice Hall.
2. Ravinshankar, A & Sathiyaseelan, A. (2022) Impact of Childhood Trauma on Psychological Distress and Personality Pathology in Young Adults. *ECS Transactions* 107(1). DOI: 10.1149/10701.3129ecst.
3. The Centre for Addiction and Mental Health. (2024). *CAMH* [online]. Trauma. Available from https://www.camh.ca/en/health-info/mental-illness-and-addic tion-index/trauma. [Accessed 8 March 2024].
4. Simon, R. A. (2016). In the Wake of Family Violence: Children, Trauma, and the Potential for Tort Litigation. *Family Advocate*, 39(2), 22–23. http://www.jstor. org/stable/26426693.
5. Jenkins, L., McNeal, T., Drayer, J. *et al.* (2021). Childhood Trauma History and Negative Social Experiences in College. *Journal of Child & Adolescent Trauma* 14, 103–113. https://doi.org/10.1007/s40653-020-00315-z.
6. Rice, F. P., & Dolgin, K. G. (2005). *The Adolescent: Development, relationships and culture* (11th ed.). Pearson Education New Zealand.
7. Seppala, E., Rossomando, T., & Doty, J. R. (2013). Social Connection and Compassion: Important Predictors of Health and Well-Being. *Social Research*, 80(2), 411–430. http://www.jstor.org/stable/24385608.

8. Bowlby, J. (1978). Attachment theory and its therapeutic implications. *Adolescent Psychiatry* 6, 5-33.

9. Alan Sroufe, L. (2005). Attachment and development: A prospective, longitudinal study from birth to adulthood. *Attachment & Human Development* 7(4), 349-367. DOI:10.1080/14616730500365928

10. Vohs, Kathleen D, & Baumeister, Roy F. (2011). *Handbook of Self-Regulation: Research, Theory and Applications* (2nd ed.). The Guilford Press.

11. Music, G. (2011). Trauma, helpfulness and selfishness: The effect of abuse and neglect on altruistic, moral and pro-social capacities. *Journal of Child Psychotherapy*, 37(2), 113-128.

12. Hershler, A. (2021). Window of Tolerance. *Looking at Trauma.* https://doi.org/10.1515/9780271092287-008.

13. Siegel, Daniel. J. (2012). *The Developing Mind* (2nd ed). The Guilford Press.

14. Arnold-de Simine. (2018). Trauma and Literature. *Trauma and Memory,* 140-152. Cambridge University Press. https://doi.org/10.1017/9781316817155.

Chapter 9

'Do You Wanna Feel How It Feels?'

Music to Heal and Harm Within the Sounds of Stranger Things

Katie Chatburn

Robin: *"Hatch said that music can reach parts of the brain that words can't. So maybe that's the key, a lifeline."*
Nancy: *"A lifeline back to reality."*
Robin: *"It's worth a shot."* (S4, E4)[1]

The original instrumental soundtrack of *Stranger Things* [2], composed by Kyle Dixon and Michael Stein, pays strong homage to 1980's composers such as Jean-Michel Jarre, John Carpenter and Giorgio Moroder through its manipulation and filtering of classic synthesisers. The resulting moody, tense soundscapes sit somewhere between the human and non-human, landing perfectly within the unique nostalgic horror vibe of the show. Alongside this soundtrack, the series features existing popular music of the 1970's and 1980's, often carefully and cleverly chosen and placed to support and enhance both characterisation and narrative. For example, Dustin and Suzie's iconic Never Ending Story duet from Season Three tells us more about their relationship whilst serving as an important example of *'audio visual dissonance'* [3], a mismatch that invites the audience to engage in a process of intellectual interaction[4]. That is, the bright and theatrical audio of the song, in contrast to the pictures of the rest of the gang being chased by monsters and variously trying to save the world, is both funny and poignant, whilst drawing us closer to the on-screen events. Arguably however, the most iconic and effective uses of popular music within the *Stranger Things* franchise are the moments in *Dear Billy* (S4, E4) where the gang enlist the help of Kate Bush to save Max from Vecna's grasp and almost certain death and Eddie's 'rooftop' moment in the Season Finale (S4, E9) as he lure's away the demobats from Creel's 'Upside Down' House.

In this chapter, we will focus on these musical moments, examining the impact of the music choices on the viewers through a range of perspectives including nostalgia, memory, and the use of music as both a weapon and a healing force.

The Soundtrack to Hawkins High

We cannot have a conversation about the soundtrack of Hawkins High without talking about "that" hill. Originally released in August 1985, Kate Bush's *Running Up That Hill (A Deal with God)*[5], from her album *Hounds of Love*, reached number 30 in the Billboard Hot 100 chart, with other top ten placements worldwide (including in the UK). The 'same' summer, in the *Stranger Things* Season Three finale, Billy is stabbed in the chest by the Mind Flayer whilst selflessly protecting Eleven. He dies in his stepsister Max's arms, shortly after apologising to her – and his death is covered up by officials as part of the Starcourt Mall fire. As viewers to this point, we might have had a difficult time trying to develop empathy for Billy. However, in this moment however, we see Billy's connection to Max, and feel sadness for the relationship that they will certainly now never experience. Much like the use of *Should I Stay Or Should I Go* (The Clash)[6], and it's important connection to Will and Jonathan Byers, the Kate Bush song (Max's favourite song) appears in various forms in Season Four, featuring reimagined versions by Rob

Simonsen and TOTEM, and becomes representative of Max's journey through her grief process during the series.

Whenever music is introduced into the soundtrack of television and film, I find myself asking why is it there and how it is shaping and manipulating how we receive the narrative? Typically, the songs on a soundtrack are an invitation to 'suspend our disbelief', as the characters are not typically hearing the music we can hear. The music then serves as a cue to viewers that *"the universe in which the events we are watching takes place is not real'* [7]. However, when the soundtrack begins to be heard by characters within the narrative, the space between real and imagined starts to morph. This use of soundtrack as heard by the on-screen characters, typically referred to as *diegetic sound*, is increasingly common in the world of contemporary soundtracks where dialogue, sound design and music often intertwine.

Early in Season Four (S4, E1) we see an example of this when Max is seen walking down the corridor of Hawkins High listening to her favourite song *Running Up That Hill (A Deal with God)*[8] on her Walkman. The music starts on Jane after her difficult presentation and subsequent slowed footage of Max begins to highlight some of the painful battles and insecurities of high school, including introducing Chrissy who becomes quickly important to the narrative. During this scene we are reminded of Max's prior relationship with Lucas as she passes him on the corridor and can almost feel her pain at this awkward and emotional interaction. The use of diegetic sound here enables us to experience Hawkins High School literally through Max's eyes and ears. We hear her favourite song through a 'shared Walkman', like an old friend, bringing us closer to her emotionally and centring her perspective, guiding the viewer as to the importance of her character's experience within the series. As humans, we often use music to help us navigate the complexities of life and make sense of difficult emotions[9] as music can trigger emotional reactions or *affective experiences* [10] . When we feel an emotion reflected in music it helps it make more 'sense' to us, we are not alone, others have felt this; it will be ok. Max is using music to control her experience of the outside world and give her the space she needs.

In fact, Max's Walkman in and of itself serves as an important vehicle for both her character and the audience to experience music throughout the show. Personal listening devices such as Walkman's create a kind of accompanied solitude[11] that allows us to manage or control our moods. Through this method of listening, Max is gaining a sense of safety, creating an audio world that feels more manageable than the one outside of it. She is working to escape the trauma of reality and navigate her emotions, *her* way. Her Walkman becomes her personal soundtrack companion through her grief experience, and as a result, becomes symbolic of the isolation she is allowing to grow between herself and the outside world. We see her distanced from her friends but we as audience are brought closer to her through this shared experience of soundtrack.

While there are many other memorable musical moments that could be explored within this chapter, we would be remiss not to talk about Eddie Munson, our underground hero, standing on the rooftop to perform Metallica's *Master of Puppets* and save his friends in the season finale of Season 4. For Eddie, who has been wrongly accused of murder and lying in hiding for much of the series, this *Master of Puppets* moment is a significant and powerful moment of redemption for his character. The song, one of Metallica's most famous, was the title track from the bands third studio album released in 1986, the year we find ourselves in within the show. As we join Eddie on top of the trailer where his horrors began, taking back sonic control of the space with his dextrous and bold guitar playing, we see him finally returned to the outlandish and alternative hero of the people that he always imagined himself to be, and we are grateful to see him back on form. Brash and driving, the song has long represented generations of angry and disenfranchised teenagers, making it the perfect anthem for Eddie's return to the helm.

In this moment we find a character that lost control of their own fate throughout much of the series spending time uncharacteristically in hiding, become celebrated and returning as a hero, pulling the 'puppet' strings and saving the day. Through diegesis and the experience of a shared soundtrack we are feeling the music *with* Eddie, we are at the gig – and just as we see Dustin nodding and smiling along, we can enjoy this moment with him, like an old friend. The swirling dark and apocalyptic imagery perfectly enhances this, as the backdrop to an impossibly great high school rock gig.

Music as a Healing Force

A key character within Season 4, Vecna, or Henry Creel's story, is initially less known to us. Throughout the season, we gradually learn more of what happened to his family, and of the false imprisonment of his father Victor whilst witnessing from the outset the psychokinetic powers he uses to target vulnerable individuals through mind control. These powers, manifesting as 'Vecna's Curse', lead his victims to experience nosebleeds, headaches, hallucinations and be overwhelmed with a fear that is difficult to resist prior to a painful death. For Max, the curse causes hallucinations of Billy and frightening journeys into the disturbing expanse of Vecna's mindscape.

The effects reach fever pitch in Episode Four; as Max's friends watch in horror as she begins to levitate and suffer the effects of a seemingly invisible torturer above Billy's grave. Meanwhile, Robin and Nancy deduce that music was playing the night of the Creel family massacre and notice how Victor hums *Dream a Little Dream of Me*[12] as he's speaking to them. The gang deduce that music could be Max's *'lifeline back to reality'* (S4, E4). Max's guilt is an evident part of her grief process and we have seen Vecna prey on those experiencing negative emotions, including guilt. Max *'feels guilty about how Billy died, that she just stood there and watched. She feels guilty that she can't tell anyone how he died, or that he died a hero — saving her and Eleven's lives. She feels guilty that they hated each other so much while he was alive* [13]. To oppose the curse it seems that opposite, more positive, feelings need to be induced.

Alongside typically inducing positive emotions[14], the power of music to heal runs deep within our systems – it has been proven to increase our bodies' level of endogenous opioid's, neurotransmitters associated with helping to decrease the stress hormone[15]. This allows the music during this key moment to bring strength to Max as her Walkman moves from a mode of disconnect to a mode of connection. We see on screen a portal opening back to the real world and the music returns her to memories of the love of her friends, as shown to us through flashbacks. She tells Vecna *'You're not really here'* and we are reminded of Luca's words *'I'm right here'* (S4, E4) as Bush sings about the moment being stolen away[16], a haunting echo of Vecna's intentions and emphasising the urgency of every passing moment.

Eventually, the resonant reminders of strength and love from the music start to bring Max the positivity she needs to counteract Vecna's attempts to prey into her vulnerable state. The strings reach a point of climax as her eyes open wide, alert and she decides to 'exchange the experience[17]' to one of living. In line with the songs title, she runs towards the portal before collapsing into Lucas' arms, echoing his words, *'I'm still here'* (E4, S4). The gang have allowed Max to find a new musically influenced perspective that draws her back to the safety of reality, a reality that she is perhaps more likely to now interact with. The shows music supervisor Nora Feldner, who was responsible for the songs placement, describes how this scene *'shows Max's strength, as she battles an actual demon as a metaphor for the strength we need to conquer our own private demons'*[18]. Through this one iconic and moving short scene, Max's inner world, Vecna's mindscape, the reality of Hawkins, Indiana and our own worlds collide; as we are reminded of our own personal traumas, both healed and yet to be healed.

Music Weaponised

Since the beginning of the *Stranger Things* franchise, the emphasis has been on the ability of the young people of Hawkins to overcome problems and fight battles using nonmainstream, often subversive means, and Season 4 is no exception. As Eddie Munson performs *Master of Puppets* [19] to lure away the demobats in the final episode of the season, we are shown yet another example of the crew claiming an autonomous non-violent method, the use of music as a tool to overcome the enemy highlighting the positive changes that can come through engaging with new, non-typical perspectives.

The song, described by the actor playing Eddie, Joe Quinn as a perfect *'smack in the face'*[20], has often been interpreted as drawing on ideas of addiction, with the master being the drug and the puppet the drug user. The shows musical supervisor connects this to Vecna as *'They share similarities in that they each have life-destroying powers that rob people of their essential personal powers'* [21]. The positioning therefore of overcoming control resonates on many levels with Eddie's journey and this moment of redemption is not lost on the audience. Rock music has historically been socially positioned as the music of the revolution and there are many examples of how rock has been used as a powerful force, from the establishment of an autonomous youth culture through rock and roll to later movements such as Rock Against Racism, the fall of the Berlin wall and the Riot Grrl movement, we are continually being shown that rock music is more than just the symbol of a disenfranchised youth - it is a powerful, noisy, collectivising weapon of societal change.

In addition, from noisy neighbours to forms of torture, rousing soldiers for battle to propaganda and intimidating enemies, *'music has always been deployed to inflame and intimidate'* [22]. There are examples from the last 30 years of ways in which popular music specifically has explicitly been used as a method of intimidation and even torture. Guantanamo detainees have described being exposed to Christina Aguilera and Eminem for long periods, sometimes while being held in stress positions[23], and during the Iraq war as troops entered Fallujah, ACDC and Metallica were blasted over loudspeakers. Ben Abel, spokesperson for the US Army's Psychological Operations Commands, explained how rock music has been weaponised *'to disorient and confuse the enemy'* [24]. With parallels to the *Stranger Things* usage, the music is chosen by the soldiers from their own personal playlists, as according to Abel *'Western music is not the Iraqis'* thing'[25].

In total contrast both to the evil, rotting imagery of Vecna and the bombastic and aggressive sounds of rock, Bush's *Running Up That Hill* brings a new perspective to the use of music as weapon. While this weaponry is not as clearly antagonistic as Eddie's use of Metallica, it is nonetheless a form of defiance through its use of the female voice. Just as *'both language and society are structured by codes of sexual difference'*[26], the voice and body are often bound by coded associations of gender, and the self-claimed feminine voice has unique social and cultural resonant connotations. The *'anchoring of the female voice in the female body confers upon it all the conventional associations of femininity with nature and matter, with emotion and irrationality'*[27] and tropes of the female voice as *'high and shrill or breathy'* have been used to *'reinforce patriarchal constructions of the feminine'*[28]. Within the Western popular music canon, these qualities have previously been captured, re-imagined, and challenged in contexts of female-led musical resistance as associated with power, embodiment and weaponization, from folk through to punk. Bush, who has been known to distance herself from the feminist label[29], is nevertheless sonically positioned *'in defiance of traditional female pop and rock singing conventions'* [30].

Music and Nostalgia

Within the many affective outcomes of music listening, 'nostalgia' is often ranked highly. The emotions that are uncovered when we listen to music depend on our prior relationship with the song and its associations[31], often these associations help us to reframe our experiences alongside creating reassuring personal continuity [32] and transporting us to other, likely preferred, times, places and memories. Eddie's performance of *Master of Puppets* perfectly aligns with his outlandish and 'larger than life' alternative persona. As Eddie returns to his true persona through this moment, the scene, and in particularly the music, reminds us of our own rebellious times, drawing on our personal nostalgic sense of youthful power and rebellion.

The Kate Bush song was released in the direct aftermath of Billy's murder and so it is unsurprising that this song is now associated with these events for Max as she has appeared 'stuck' in reflection and nostalgic thought in relation to what happened to Billy the previous summer. The song becomes representative of her gaining strength as she works through the grief process and she uses these associations of strength, via the medium of her personal audio world, to transport herself 'back' to a 'better' time and place and connect her to a preferred (and safer) reality within Hawkins.

The impact of this scene, and particular song, also extend far beyond Max's experience and it is in later years and for wider audiences than Max that we can truly see the role of nostalgia in relation to Bush's release. In 2022, within a year of international lockdowns due to the COVID-19 pandemic, the song was more successful than its release 37 years prior due to the propulsion of the *Stranger Things* placement. The song made it to no. 3 in The Hot 100 charts and number one in several other worldwide charts (including the UK), reaching one billion streams on Spotify by June 2023.

This song, alongside *Master of Puppets*, clearly evokes a sense of nostalgia for individuals worldwide, through the lens of a franchise which has connected people back to their 80's upbringings whilst shining a new light on the era for those born later, emphasising the importance of pop music and nostalgia for both audiences [33]. The 80's resurgence of the last few years has included the return of the cassette tape which symbolizes *'love, human connection, the oddball rebel, and authenticity'* [34], connecting directly both to Max's character and story and the nostalgic yearning of audiences experiencing a *'sentimental yearning for positive aspects of one's past'* [35]. This attachment to real or imagined 'better times' is of special poignancy during this time with research highlighting a 'nostalgic bump' during the pandemic period and individuals gravitating to a place of reassurance to help them deal with the social isolation [36]. Immediately post pandemic, much of the social landscape was permanently altered, further emphasising a need to 'cling' to nostalgic memories of a preferred prior existence.

Music, Memory, and Time

It is unsurprising that the series producers chose an experience based on musical memory as Max's tool of protection due to the wealth of research that highlights how it can be preserved, even during the impact of neurological diseases. Music has also been used to aid medical recovery across a range of contexts for many decades, with an early documented case showing a physician using music within the context of surgery as early as 1914[37]. Musical memory is encoded and preserved within the brain in unique ways[38], as demonstrated through patients suffering from amnesia who have been found to be able to preserve musical memory, and dementia research which shows that despite the impairment caused by the disease on the hippocampal pathway, musical memories can be preserved into the very late stages of the disease's development[39]. Many contemporary research studies continue to highlight the importance of music within these contexts, including a 2008 study demonstrating that stroke patients who listened to their favourite music for a couple of hours a day post recovery showed improvement in symptoms of depression, confusion, verbal memory, and focused attention[40]. As Dr Hatch tells us during Nancy and Robin's tour of one of the more popular areas of the asylum in which Creel is incarcerated, the Listening Room, *'the right song, particularly one which holds some personal meaning, can prove a salient stimulus'* (S4, E4).

The overall dark and dramatic quality of *Running Up That Hill*, is, like much of Bush's work, tinged by an operatic quality that moves outside of typical pop music forms into an *'authentically progressive'* [41], sound world. This expansive world seems to move beyond ideas of memory and time towards something that cannot be easily placed. Bush is known to experiment sonically, using *'ancient musical instruments, like the dijeridu and the bouzouki, with their earthy tones, alongside modern instruments like the electric guitar and the Fairlight'*[42]. The Fairlight CMI digital sampler is fundamental to the creation of *Running Up That Hill* and was created, in Australia, only a few years prior to the songs release in 1979, its invention presented a world of possibilities and unlimited sound which *'literally changed the course of music'* [43], influencing many of the sounds of the 80's era and beyond. Bush's *Running Up That Hill* is comprised almost completely from sounds of the Fairlight II, dreaming up new and 'other worldly' sounds and resonating with Bush's recurring lyrical theme of the *'interconnectedness of past, present, and future'* [44]. This sits perfectly with a drama that largely exists in other worlds and plays with timeframes, narratively moving between the past and present interspersed with future premonition. The song choice also bridges the various worlds of Hawkins and the reality of its contemporary audiences, resonating through its powerful nostalgic qualities.

The music video for *Running Up That Hill* shows Kate and her dance partner Michael Hervieu, performing 'complex moves that seemed both embracing and combative' [45] which feels symbolic of Max and Billy's relationship. We wonder perhaps if there is something of Max that wishes she could go back in time and swap places with Billy, giving him the chance to live instead of her [46]. These ideas connect with a slightly darker air within the song, drawing out the ritualistic elements which include a drum beat that gives us the sense of 'raising the dead' through its shamanistic and repetitive quality. A deal with God here begins to sound more like a deal with the Devil, highlighting the songs resonances *'of a dark magickal act'* [47]. This devilish trade for Billy's life does not feel outside the internal logic of a series about the rituals of teen hood, that *'utilizes inventive takes on horror tropes and the supernatural'* [48], as it continues to experiment with, but not completely reveal, the unknown qualities and possibilities of the Upside Down.

Concluding Thoughts

As demonstrated, the choice of *Running Up That Hill* for this moment in Series Four has multiple layers of meaning within the narrative. From Max's connection to Billy, to Lucas and to the rest of her friends and beyond, the song acts as the perfect medium to say what words sometimes cannot: perfect for a character who is not known for verbal soliloquies. In addition, *'let's be real: It's also perfect running-through-a-hellscape-of-falling-debris music'* [49], the combination of this visual and audio is undoubtably a highly iconic moment within the franchise. This choice, alongside Eddie's iconic *Master of Puppets* moment, not only serves as a reminder for many of us of our teenage years and connection to our treasured album collection, but of the important role that music continually plays in helping us to navigate, colour and remember our experience of the world and our interactions with others. This use of music and its effect on us throughout the series reminds us that this is a story about friendship, connection, and love - what happens when we withdraw from it or lose it and how good it feels to get it back.

As is often the case with well-written drama, Stranger *Things* asks bigger questions of its audiences than might be first apparent from the immediate on-screen action. The negativity and isolation of Henry Creel and the creation of Vecna, as associated with disintegrating landscapes and rotting, intestinal imagery, is counteracted by the heroic actions of Eddie as he reclaims physical and sonic territory through his musical moment on the roof. Perhaps through use of immediately rebellious, and for many nostalgic soundtracks, imploring us to remember the power that exists in all of us and calling us towards our own rooftop revolution?

There are also lessons to be learnt from the way that the loving instincts that bring Max into a more positive frame of mind act as a powerful weapon against her own demise. Music supervisor Felder describes how Max is 'running' literally and figuratively, *'from an evil representation of the absence of love, and towards the overwhelming care and understanding so powerfully shown by her friends'* [50], a path paved perfectly by a song about seeing another's perspective. She says *'I think it's struck a chord for so many people because it really touches on the alienation and emotional struggle that so many of us go through at one point or another in life, especially as teenagers. Music gives us validation and strength, especially when we aren't feeling supported or understood by others*[51]. So, in asking, *'Do you wanna feel how it feels?'* [52] The use of Metallica and Kate Bush within the season remind us of our individual struggles and of the wider implications of connection, as, in the words of Will *'that's what holds this whole party together. heart...without heart, we'd all fall apart.'* (S4, E8).

---

1. Dichter, P., (Writer), & Levy, S., (Director). (2022., May 27). Dear Billy (Season Four, Episode Four) [TV Series Episode]. In Shawn Levy (Executive Producer). *Stranger Things.* 21 Laps Entertainment.
2. Shawn Levy (Executive Producer). (2016). *Stranger Things* [TV Series]. 21 Laps Entertainment.
3. Kruth, P. and Stobart, H. (2007) *Sound.* Cambridge University Press. p. 219
4. Lipscomb, S. D. and Kendall, R. A. (1994). Perceptual judgement of the relationship between musical and visual components in film, *Psychomusicology: A Journal of Research in Music Cognition,* 13(1-2), pp.60-98
5. Bush, K. (1985). Running Up That Hill (A Deal With God) [Song]. On *Hounds of Love.* EMI.
6. The Clash. (1981). Should I Stay or Should I Go [Song]. On *Combat Rock.* CBS; Epic.
7. Winters, B. (2010). The non-diegetic fallacy: Film, music, and narrative space, *Music and Letters,* 91(2), pp. 224-244.
8. Bush, K. (1985). *Running Up That Hill* (A Deal With God) [Song]. On *Hounds of Love.* EMI.
9. Viskontas, I. (2019). *How Music Can Make You Better.* The HOW Series: Chronicle Books.
10. Ren, W.-H. (2000). Library instruction and college student self-efficacy in electronic information searching, *The Journal of Academic Librarianship,* 26(5), pp. 323-328.
11. Bull, M. (2006) Investigating the culture of mobile listening: From Walkman to iPod, *Consuming music together: Social and collaborative aspects of music consumption technologies:* Springer, pp. 134
12. Louis Armstrong and Ella Fitzgerald (1950). *Dream A Little Dream of Me* [Song]. Decca

13. Maravegias, J. (2022) *Music Soothes Our Savage Minds: Kate Bush's Effect On 'Stranger Things'*. Pajiba: Pajiba [Website]. Available at: https://www.pajiba.com/tv_reviews/music-soothes-our-savage-minds-kate-bushs-effect-on-stranger-things.php (Accessed: 24th March 2024).

14. Lundqvist, L.-O., Carlsson, F., Hilmersson, P. and Juslin, P. (2009) Emotional responses to music: Experience, expression, and physiology, *Psychology of Music*, 37, pp. 61-90.

15. Viskontas, I. (2019) *How Music Can Make You Better*. The HOW Series: Chronicle Books.

16. Bush, K. (1985). *Running Up That Hill* (A Deal With God) [Song]. On *Hounds of Love*. EMI.

17. ibid

18. Bitran, T. and DiLillo, J. (2023) *Why Max's Favorite Song on 'Stranger Things' Is Now No. 1 on iTunes*. Tudum: Netflix [Review Website]. Available at: https://www.netflix.com/tudum/articles/this-is-the-stranger-things-song-everyone-is-talking-about (Accessed: 11th March 2024 2024).

19. Metallica. 1986. Master of Puppets [Song]. On *Master of Puppets*. Elektra.

20. Bitran, T. (2022) *Quinn on his 'badass' Metallica Solo in the Stranger Things Finale*. Tudum: Netflix [Review Website]. Available at: https://www.netflix.com/tudum/articles/eddie-munson-metallica-master-of-puppets-stranger-things (Accessed: 11th March 2024 2024).

21. Tangcay, J. (2022) *How Stranger Things Landed Metallica's Master of Puppets for Epic Finale*. Variety [website]. Available at: https://variety.com/2022/artisans/news/stranger-things-metallica-master-of-puppets-1235307853/ (Accessed: 11th March 2024 2024).
    Bitran, T. (2022) *Quinn on his 'badass' Metallica Solo in the Stranger Things Finale*. Tudum: Netflix [Review Website]. Available at: https://www.netflix.com/tudum/articles/eddie-munson-metallica-master-of-puppets-stranger-things (Accessed: 11th March 2024 2024).

22. Cloonan, M. and Johnson, B. (2002) Killing me softly with his song: An initial investigation into the use of popular music as a tool of oppression, *Popular Music*, 21(1), pp. 27-39.

23. Cusick, S. G. (2020) 'Music as torture/Music as weapon', *The Auditory Culture Reader*: Routledge, pp. 379-391.

24. DeGregory, L. (2005) 'Iraq 'n' Roll', *Tampa Bay Times*. Available at: https://www.tampabay.com/archive/2004/11/21/iraq-n-roll/ (Accessed: 11the March 2024).

25. ibid

26. Dunn, L. C. and Jones, N. A. (1994) *Embodied voices: Representing female vocality in Western culture*. Cambridge University Press. P. 3

27. ibid

28. ibid

29. Forrest, B. (2023) ''Room For The Life': Kate Bush's misunderstood "feminist" anthem', *Far Out*.

30. Kruse, H (1999). Gender. In *Key Concepts in Popular Music and Culture*. Ed. Horner, B and Swiss, T. Oxford: Blackwell Publishing. p.90

31. Barrett, F. S., Grimm, K. J., Robins, R. W., Wildschut, T., Sedikides, C., & Janata, P. (2010). Music-evoked nostalgia: Affect, memory, and personality. *Emotion*, 10(3), 390–403.

32. Seigworth, G. (2003) 'Fashioning a stave, or, singing life', *Animations of Deleuze and Guattari*, 1, p. 85

33. Glennon, H. (2023) 'Genre Theory and Stranger Things: Breaking Boundaries, Nostalgia, and the Pop Culture Influence', *Mise-en-scene*, 8(1).

34. Galvin, K. (2020) 'Tracking hypernostalgia: Soundtrack albums and the return of the cassette in American film and television', *The Soundtrack Album*: Routledge, pp. 190-208.

35. Sedikides, C., Leunissen, J. and Wildschut, T. (2021). The psychological benefits of music-evoked nostalgia', *Psychology of Music*, 50(6), pp. 2044-2062.

36. Huang, K.-J., Chang, Y.-H. and Landau, M. J. (2024). Pandemic nostalgia: Reduced social contact predicts consumption of nostalgic music during the COVID-19 pandemic, *Social Psychological and Personality Science*, 15(1), pp. 12-21.

37. Taylor, Dale B., (1981),'Music in General Hospital Treatment from 1900 to 1950', *Journal of Music Therapy*, XVIII (2), pp.. 62-73.

38. Jacobsen, J.-H., Stelzer, J., Fritz, T. H., Chételat, G., La Joie, R. and Turner, R. (2015). Why musical memory can be preserved in advanced Alzheimer's disease, *Brain*, 138(8), pp. 2439

39. ibid

40. Sarkamo, T., et al. (2008) Music Listening Enhances Cognitive Recovery and Mood after Middle Cerebral Artery Stroke, *Brain*, vol. 131, no. 3, pp. 866–76. *DOI.org* (*Crossref*), https://doi.org/10.1093/brain/awno13.

41. Hegarty, P. and Halliwell, M. (2021). *Beyond and Before, Updated and Expanded Edition: Progressive Rock Across Time and Genre*. Bloomsbury Publishing USA. P.259

42. ibid

43. The Sydney Morning Herald. (2022, August 25). *How The Fairlight CMI Changed The Course of Music*. YouTube. https://www.youtube.com/watch?v=jkiYyoi8FtA&t=648s

44. Kruse, H. (1999). Gender. In Key Concepts in Popular Music and Culture. Ed. Horner, B and Swiss, T. Oxford: Blackwell Publishing, (p. 90)

45. Doyle, T. (2022) *Running Up That Hill 50 Visions of Kate Bush*. Blink Publishing. P.45

46. Maravgis, J. (2022) *Music Soothes Our Savage Minds: Kate Bush's Effect On 'Stranger Things'*. Pajiba: Pajiba [Website]. Available at: https://www.pajiba.com/tv_reviews/music-soothes-our-savage-minds-kate-bushs-effect-on-stranger-things.php (Accessed: 24th March 2024).

47. Doyle, T. (2022) *Running Up That Hill 50 Visions of Kate Bush*. Blink Publishing. p.25

48. Glennon, H. (2023) 'Genre Theory and Stranger Things: Breaking Boundaries, Nostalgia, and the Pop Culture Influence', *Mise-en-scene*, 8(1).

49. Bitran., T. and DiLillo J. (2023). *Why Max's Favorite Song on 'Stranger Things' Is Now No. 1 on iTunes*. Tudum: Netflix [Review Website]. Available at:

https://www.netflix.com/tudum/articles/this-is-the-stranger-things-song-every-one-is-talking-about#:~:text=In%20Episode%204%2C%20"Dear%20Billy,her%20friends%2C"%20says%20Felder (Accessed: 11th March 2024).

50. Bitran., T. and DiLillo., J. (2023) *Why Max's Favorite Song on 'Stranger Things' Is Now No. 1 on iTunes*. Tudum: Netflix [Review Website]. Available at: https://www.netflix.com/tudum/articles/this-is-the-stranger-things-song-every-one-is-talking-about#:~:text=In%20Episode%204%2C%20"Dear%20Billy,her%20friends%2C"%20says%20Felder (Accessed: 11th March 2024).

51. ibid

52. Bush, K., 1985. Running Up That Hill (A Deal With God) [Song]. On *Hounds of Love*. EMI.

About the Editor

Anton Roberts is a criminology/sociology researcher at the Policy Evaluation and Research Unit (PERU) at Manchester Metropolitan University (MMU) in the UK. In his day-to-day work, he is involved in various program evaluations relating to the criminal justice system with a focus on youth crime and what factors drive or reduce rates of reoffending. Anton is also currently studying for his PhD – looking at the intersection of gender/hyper-masculinity (harmful forms of gender) in the homelessness community, here in Manchester. In addition, he also produces the 'Backstage Academic' Podcast, a none pay walled platform designed to amplify the voices of early researchers and interview academic authors. Finally, Anton is a writer/presenter in the making of factual documentaries that applies a sociologic lens to contemporary issues such as violence and forms of extremism. His favorite character is Murray Bauman because despite being unapologetically anti-social his understanding and wit are second to none.

About The Authors

Saiqa Butt is a writer, editor and general creative tidy-upper - having worked with published authors, academia and creatives to support them in their work and help them in their quest (some would call it an obsession) of finding the perfect word, sentence and/or coffee. Although based in Manchester, Saiqa is an intrepid and worryingly clumsy explorer, falling onto beaches, pavements, and many other cemented surfaces around the world. Her bruises are now sectioned via continent. Splitting her time supporting authors and academics with their writing/ editing, running creative workshops for people experiencing homelessness and addiction, and studying psychology, Saiqa occasionally finds time to attempt some writing of her own. Her writing centres around mythology, the supernatural, and explores themes of culture and identity. Saiqa was born in Germany, to Indian, Pakistani and Tanzanian parents, - and describes her formative years, and her sense of identity, as "bloody confusing" – a feeling that has permeated her adult life leading to a consistent state of enjoyable chaos. Splitting her time supporting authors and academics with their writing/ editing, running creative workshops for people experiencing homelessness and addiction, and studying psychology, Saiqa occasionally finds time to attempt some writing of her own. Her writing centres around mythology, the supernatural, and explores themes of culture and identity.

Katie Chatburn is a composer, arranger / orchestrator and academic, in 2016 she was awarded Associate of the Royal Academy of

Music for her work within the music industry. In 2017 Katie formed Ignition Orchestra as conductor and arranger. Following their debut at Liverpool International Festival, the orchestra has performed to sell out audiences at venues including The Barbican, Royal Festival Hall and The Royal Albert Hall, appeared on the Graham Norton Show and released an album with Sony as part of the Garage Classical project. Further credits for arrangements and orchestrations include work for the BBC, Channel 4 and ITV, including original music for Radio 4 and Radio 3 drama. Katie has worked with artists including The Sugababes, Paloma Faith, Sigma, Lady Blackbird, Aloe Blacc, Sigma and Mike Skinner. Katie lectures part time at the Royal Northern College of Music and is currently studying a Leverhulme Trust funded PhD at Manchester Metropolitan University looking at the role of sound in urban environments.

Holly Hawkes born in the south of England, studied Criminology and Forensic Science at Manchester Metropolitan University, MA Gender and Sexuality at The University of Manchester, and is currently researching for an EdD at Huddersfield University specialising in young women, neurodiversity, and disciplinary policies while working as a teacher of criminology in Further Education. Diagnosed as autistic later in life, Holly has lived with a fascination for performance and understanding the variances in the expression of emotion in everyday life as well as on-screen and on stage. Research interests include media from a sociological and psychological perspective, as well as social justice and education. Other interests include the impact of media, media analysis, music and gaming from a personal perspective, and also their uses, benefits, and how they are critiqued in the media. Her favorite character from *Stranger Things* is Eddie as he represents the struggles of many alternative people, not only of the era but still today.

Jennifer Russell, LMSW is a Supervisee of Social Work with a graduate certificate from Georgetown University in Infant and Early

Childhood Mental Health. She provides play-based therapeutic services to children 0-12 and their families. She has a special interest in the therapeutic use of video games and tabletop role playing games and incorporates both into clinical practice when appropriate. When she is not focused on dismantling the barriers of access to children's mental health services or stressing about upcoming military moves, she enjoys reading, cozy gaming, and spending time with her husband, three boys, and two dogs. Her favorite character from *Stranger Things* is Bob Newby as he was the epitome of being a good human and she will forever grieve him.

Neil Stafford is a licensed psychologist working in his private practice, Desert Rain Health and Wellbeing, in the west valley of Phoenix, AZ. His practice provides individual and group therapy working across the lifespan with a focus on treating depression and anxiety. Dr. Stafford is an expert evaluator for learning disabilities and autism. He is married with 2 boys, ages 8 and 11. They are all Arizona natives living in the Litchfield Park area. Dr. Stafford has been a lifelong geek with a love for Star Trek and Dungeons and Dragons beginning in childhood. He has been an avid gamer since adolescence with his first NES. Now he enjoys sci-fi and fantasy books and shows as well as gaming with his kids and friends. Dr. Stafford worked at Avondale Elementary School District (AESD) 18 years providing psychological services to children ages 5 to 15. He is board certified in School Psychology by the American Board of Professional Psychology. He was the Special Education Director for 6 of those years. Dr. Stafford then served for 1 year as Clinical Director for Axis for Autism. He continues to work part time for Axis as an evaluator. Dr. Stafford has served on several community service and professional association governing and advisory boards. He was the 2021 President of the Arizona Psychological Association. AZPA has awarded him the Early Career Psychologist, Mentor of the Year, and Distinguished Service Awards. His favorite character in *Stranger things* is Hopper as they are in the same stage in life and can see himself in him protecting and mentoring others.

Chloe Stollery holds a BA (Hons) Contemporary Theatre and Performance and MEd Psychology of Education. Professionally, she has dedicated my career to supporting special educational needs within various educational contexts. She has spent the last four years of her career leading the Social, Emotional and Mental Health provision within a trust of schools. She provides specialist behaviour support for both staff and students, to support greater outcomes for children with complex developmental behaviour differences. She is passionate to support developing young people to become better communicators and feels strongly about providing advocacy whilst supporting them to do this. Her favorite character in *Stranger Things* is Max Mayfield. She's blunt, brooding, and able to communicate a storyline with just a few words.

Isobelle Whinnett is halfway through a part-time practice based PhD in creative writing. As a creative practitioner, her work is in Young Adult genre fiction exploring themes such as grief, identity and sisterhood. As a researcher, her work examines the connection between queer women's narratives in Fantasy Gothic literature and the use of monsters, foregrounding the figures of the Witch and the Ghost. Her research centres on evolving queer narratives and treatment in Young Adult fiction. Isobelle will begin as a part-time lecturer in January 2024, teaching two units, 'Academic Practice 2' and 'Approaches to Creative Writing'. Her favorite character in *Stranger Things* is Max Mayfield because who doesn't relate to their favorite song on repeat being a savior from certain death.

About Play Story Press

https://playstorypress.org/about/
Play Story Press™ is an open community publishing consortium of/by/for the field and our community. It is a diamond open-access academic publishing initiative in which contributors retain all their intellectual property. We work with our contributors in as timely a manner as possible so that we can share ideas that have impact and significance in our society.

Play Story Press is a culmination of 20 years of open-access publishing and collaborating with the community. Our founders started ETC Press in 2005 as an experimental open-access academic publishing imprint, and our success was a direct result of all the quality work written by our community. Inspired by this, Play Story Press is evolving to focus more on the community and field. The consortium comprises an exceptional group of partner organizations that will work together, shaping and supporting Play Story Press for the field and community.

Publishing with Play Story Press is a friendly, supportive and constructive process focused on encouraging the growth of quality scholarship in this field. Play Story Press is committed to publishing three types of work: peer-reviewed work (research-based books, text-books, academic journals, conference proceedings), general audience work (trade nonfiction, singles, Well Played singles), and research and white papers. The common thread among these is a focus on issues related to stories and play as they are applied across various fields.

The concepts of story and play are broad and diverse—from

entertainment and narrative to media studies and social studies, games and technology to health and enjoyment, education and learning to design and development, and more. Our authors come from a range of backgrounds. Some are traditional academics. Some are practitioners. And some work in between. Their ability to write about the impact of play and story and their significance in society ties them all together.

In keeping with our mission, Play Story Press uses emerging technologies to design all our books and on-demand publishers to distribute our e-books and print books through all the major retail chains, such as Amazon, Barnes & Noble, Kobo, and Apple. We also work with The Game Crafter to produce tabletop games.

We publish books but are also interested in the participatory future of content creation across multiple media. We are exploring what it means to publish across multiple media and versions. We believe this is the future of publishing, bridging virtual and physical media with fluid versions of publications and enabling the creative blurring of what constitutes reading and writing.

We don't carry an inventory ourselves. Instead, each print book is created when somebody buys a copy. Since the Play Story Press is an open-access publisher, every book, journal, and proceeding is available as a free download, we're partnering with open-access supporters to host our online repository, and we price our titles as inexpensively as possible because we want people to have access to them. We're most interested in the sharing and spreading of ideas. Authors retain ownership of their intellectual property. We release our books, journals, and proceedings under a Creative Commons license.

Play Story Press™ is an independent non-profit organization powered by input and involvement from the consortium, our contributors, and the community at large. This continues our innovations in publishing, and we invite people to participate. Together, we can explore and create the future of open academic publishing, sharing and spreading ideas and knowledge that can help change the world for the better.